THE MAGDALENE MISSION

A Modern-Day Search for the Missing Pages
of the Gospel of Mary

KEN FRY

THE MAGDALENE MISSION
Copyright © 2023 KEN FRY

All Rights Reserved

No part of this publication may be reproduced, distributed, or transmitted in any form or by any means, including photocopying, recording, or other electronic or mechanical methods, without the prior written permission of the publisher, except in the case of brief quotations embodied in critical reviews and certain other noncommercial uses permitted by copyright law.

This is a work of fiction. Names, characters, businesses, places, events, and incidents are either the products of the author's imagination or used in a fictitious manner. Any resemblance to actual persons, living or dead, or actual events is purely coincidental.

www.booksbykenfry.com

BOOKS BY KEN FRY
MYSTERY SUSPENSE THRILLERS

Editing, Cover Design and Formatting by The Book Khaleesi
www.thebookkhaleesi.com

ACKNOWLEDGEMENTS

I would like to extend my appreciation to my esteemed Book Manager, Eeva Lancaster, and her hardworking team. Their support has been invaluable in what has been a difficult patch for me...

Finally, a big thank you to *you*, my readers and followers, for your support and reviews. Truly you have made this a remarkable journey.

More tales on their way! Happy reading.

Ken Fry
Surrey, UK

BOOKS by KEN FRY

BESTSELLING NOVELS

The Keeper's Cup
The Patmos Enigma: Quest of the Wandering Jew
The Lazarus Succession

THE LAZARUS MYSTERIES
(Duology)

The Lazarus Succession
The Lazarus Continuum
The Lazarus Mysteries: Omnibus Collection
La Sucesión Lazaro

THE LADY CRUSADER SERIES
(Trilogy)

The Chronicles of Aveline: Awakening
The Chronicles of Aveline: Love and Blood
The Chronicles of Aveline: The Final Sacrifice

SUSPENSE THRILLERS
(Standalone Novels)

Shakyamuni's Pearl
Red Ground: The Forgotten Conflict
The Brodsky Affair
Suicide Seeds

BITE-SIZED THRILLS

Looks Can Be Misleading
Check Mate
The Long Case Clock (FREE)

CONTEMPORARY FICTION

Drunks: An Alcoholic Drama
Dying Days

AUDIOBOOKS

The Keeper's Cup
The Chronicles of Aveline: Awakening
The Chronicles of Aveline: Love and Blood
(Book 2)
The Chronicles of Aveline: Final Sacrifice
(Book 3)
The Lazarus Succession
The Lazarus Continuum
The Brodsky Affair
The Patmos Enigma
Red Ground: The Forgotten Conflict
Drunks: An Alcoholic Drama

Available on Audible

Mary Magdalene by Piero di Cosimo
Wikimedia Commons

Chapter 1

*A Street in Magdala
Judea 14 CE*

Mary wearily awoke and once more felt puzzled. She stretched tight arms and fingers as she recalled her recurring dream, which was repeating itself more frequently. She had rolled around all night in her bed without feeling any easier. Her vision was of a faraway place of which she knew nothing.

She sensed it and could comprehend it as an ancient sacred building but knew not where it was. She could tell that the inhabitants were religious. The manner of their dress told her so. Their heads were shaven, and they wore thick robes coloured maroon and orange. With them was the vista and touch of cold snow, kept at bay by a watery yellow sun. They were not priests, such as Jerusalem's rabbis, or Romans as she had sometimes seen them making sacrifices to their strange gods.

In the quietness of her simple room, her long coppery hair fell about her shoulders, as if Elah himself had draped it upon them. Struggling in her mind was a sense of a paradoxical

THE MAGDALENE MISSION

attraction to what she could only vaguely see. There was a beauty about it that caused her heart to hurt. It called to her. Love and longing enfolded her in a feeling of deep kindness. She had never felt this before. It possessed an immensity of love beyond anything on earth she had known. It exceeded that of her mother and father's.

Facial features in the dream were but a blur. In her ears were faint whisperings. What was being said was not understandable, but the unknown sounds gave a gentle comfort. If understood, she felt her knowledge would increase and guide her to greater intimacy with the words of Elah. That was how profound they seemed. Why should she think this? There was no way of knowing. The unknown had forever fascinated her. At her young age came an uncertain intuitiveness that could only be considered mystical, a secret path to a greater understanding of Elah. This thought was kept to herself. For women, let alone young girls, to think or speak of such things was abhorrent to many men and priests.

The idea came dawning that she should inform her parents of the dreams. There could be no others she could talk with. Would they be able to help her understand? To wait and see was the only answer.

She had no idea what to make of the dreams, yet even in their strangeness there was a deep familiarity with what flitted through her mind. In them were contained warmth, knowledge, and a feeling of safety, which she sensed swathing through her entire being. Any attempt to reach out and touch it caused only grasping at handfuls of empty air. Each time the dream appeared, more details became revealed. Specifics of location, structure, and the hidden faces of the participants were inching towards the identifiable. She had now found herself wanting to see more clearly, although caution remained.

What was being told to her? There was no way of knowing, and that was unnerving. Reaching out to her came the unknown. It had a personal quality and possessed a loving intimacy of what she sensed was being extended to her.

❦

The names Mary and Miriam were common in the neighbourhood of Magdala and so as to know who she was, Mary was often called by the name Magdalene. She became known and referred to as *the* Magdalene. Already she stood as high as her father's chin and reached almost her mother's height. Magdalene was slender, not a beauty as most men desired, but possessed of a captivating demeanour. Her hair colour was unusual in those parts. Her facial features were wide and honest, with high cheekbones topped with vivid green eyes, which were an added rarity to Magdalene's appearance. At thirteen years of age, when she stretched her long slender arms above her head and stood to her full height, she could touch the white roof. In her blossoming years and condition, she was considered a woman and soon to be ready for marriage, as a while back her menses had begun. Her red hair, most unusual in Galilee and indeed the entire land of Judea, often brought much comment, some good and some not so. Her blessed body was graced with smooth olive skin. That was not unusual, but those strange green eyes often caused derision, even fear, but also admiration amongst the locals. Many boys found the Magdalene to their liking. Magdalene found no interest in them. With her family, she lived a humble life in a typical dwelling in the tiny town.

THE MAGDALENE MISSION

Taking up a bedding mat, Magdalene would often make her way to the roof to sleep when the weather became too hot. On these nights, she would take her beloved kinnor with her and across its ten strings play and gently sing old Hebrew psalms. Gazing up, she would sing to the vastness of the night sky and countless stars that stretched in a bejewelled goodness and seemingly had no end. Its beauty and size would bring her to tears and somehow, she felt part of it, and that it was part of her being too. A sense of oneness would overwhelm her and also cause her to gasp out loud. It was inexplicable.

The walls of their house were of white stucco and there were three small rooms. At night, they kept their chickens and two goats in the rear room. Her mother, Ruth, a no-nonsense but loving mother, was a respected member of the local community and reputed to look after and guard the family well. She did all that was needed to keep them well-fed and cared for. Now in her middle years, her looks had begun gently fading like dawn putting the stars to flight. Once lustrous dark hair had begun greying, and her face was tiring. All she cared for was the welfare and happiness of her family. She was not unaware of the reactions her daughter attracted. It gave her cause to think of the inhumanity of people to others who were not the same as them.

Are we not all children of Elah? Why do people behave so cruelly?

Joshua was Ruth's husband. He was taller than all the others around him, and his features were brown, and beginning to wrinkle. His eyes had that faint green mist about them, which he had passed on to Mary. It gave him an esteemed and influential air. He had married late and was now an elder in the community. He worked as his father before him had done as a dyer of fabrics and a tailor of cloth. He was well regarded and there were few days when he was not busy. Their colourful street was full of the varied noises and cries of merchants, sellers of goods, craftsmen of all sorts, fabric weavers, tailors, stonemasons, builders, carpenters, iron and steel workers, and indeed anything that served a useful human purpose. It was a bustling and busy town. Amongst the tradespeople there existed a common bond of respect and a willingness to live harmoniously together – with the odd few exceptions, as in any community. As for Magdalene, she had only a few close friends and nobody as an intimate confidante. Many saw her as being strange, mature for her years, aloof, and never too sociable or as willing to play as the others. Those who knew her would say otherwise. They found her compassionate and caring, with a degree of understanding well beyond her years.

She cared not.

Magdalene's thoughts and ideas were beyond what she heard in the streets and alleyways of Magdala. Something deeper, she sensed, was contained in life's meaning. That thought was constantly calling. Its voice she felt with a secret intensity. Many hours were spent just asking herself, over and over the questions... *what, who, why am I?*

These thoughts were deeply troubling. Her moods became more solitary, and she became less able to mix and spend free time with others.

"C'mon Mary, we are going down to the sea to watch the fish being caught," her sister Martha shouted at her.

It was as if Magdalene had not heard her. She was gazing, with a deep contemplative expression etched across her face, into the nearby stretch of undulating hills. A shake of her head gave Martha her answer. Standing up, she tightened the cincture of her outer tunic, and adjusted the head cover. She could smell its freshly washed scent and feel the soft comfort of its texture around her hair.

She headed through the welcome shade of the green olive grove and on towards the hills, making her way upwards without another word. She knew not why but felt compelled to do so.

The dust-covered track leading into the hills shimmered under the heat of an unforgiving, impersonal, scorching yellow sun. The ground looked brown, parched, and barren. All around was only suffocating grime, sand, and struggling green growth and potential olives. Starting out, she could hear the birds singing, as they always seemed to when her walks began. She liked to think they did so because it was their salutation to her unknown quest. They were encouraging her to keep on the investigative path and not to stray from it.

Here and there survived dull-green bushes and wilting shrubs, but pitifully few. Dotted around, as always, flourished sturdy palm trees. This was a walk she had been undertaking more of late. The quietness of the hills had an attraction, and it was here, away from the town's clamour, that Magdalene could allow her mind to drift.

The hills embraced her with a hidden mystery that pierced the very marrow of her bones. It was unsayable, unspeakable, but it was there, and it was for her. This she knew with no uncertainty.

In quieter moments, Magdalene fancied she heard their whisperings, which echoed her frequent dreams. What she was experiencing she knew not, but in her mind their familiarity contained a message of love and peace. Within them was an unknowable majesty she could not grasp.

It was then there appeared a figure, approaching her from

the hazy light of the summit. Coming into view, she recognised it as the boy she knew to be Yeshua. Although his hometown of Nazareth was miles away, at least a day and a half or more of travel, he would often appear with Joseph – his father, the carpenter – to do work. He stood taller than her and had compelling eyes of deep brown that were the same colour as his long hair. His mother's name was also Mary, often called Mary the Nazarene. Yeshua and Magdalene had spoken with each other occasionally, and he generated a sense of warm wisdom and confidence. At times, she had noticed him gazing at her with a thoughtful expression and a quiet smile. She had long sensed he was not like the others and had developed a liking for him. There were stories about him, that he was wiser than the priests and rabbis and would often confound them during debates and discussions at the temple in Jerusalem. Some even said he made stricken, injured birds able to fly again just by holding and whispering to them.

They drew close and, when near, they both came to a stop. Facing each other, there was a silence between them. She felt no shyness, nor did she look away. There was a presence about him that was comforting and compelling,

He gave her a reassuring smile, brushed the billowing dust from his hooded chitōn, and spoke. "I am pleased to meet you here, Magdalene, for there's something I've been wanting to speak of with you."

What in Elah's name could that be? "You want to speak to *me* of something, Yeshua? Have I done something wrong?"

"No, Magda, you have not. There's much about you that shows you understand and know more than most. Your heart is good, and it shines from you. I know that soon I shall be far from this place once the Festival of Pesach is done. Where I am going, I know not, but it will be a long distance from here.

I shall not be seen or heard of for many years. All I know is that… you alone will find me."

"Yeshua, what are you talking about? This is nonsense. I am going nowhere, nor are you. We belong here."

"We belong everywhere, Magda – Jerusalem, Galilee, Magdala, or anywhere on this earth. All men shall know. You will see and you will understand." He stood back from her puzzled face. "Now I must be on my way. The festival is soon to begin, and I have to be there. I know not when we'll meet again, but it will be."

To her surprise, he moved closer, held her by the arms, and for a brief moment gazed into her eyes, then leant forward and kissed her forehead before making his way back to town.

Magdalene stopped her walk and sat down upon a large white rock. The kiss had been startling, and her heart raced.

A tingling sensation passed through her entire being and her mind sang a song of joy.

For reasons unfathomable, there was no doubting the inherent truth she felt about his words. There was no uncertainty. Why? She had no idea. The manner of his words possessed an undeniable quality that, for her, moved towards an inevitability that had no way of being stopped.

A thought arose in her, from where she had no idea. *Eyes closed, see your inner being in detail. Thus see your true nature.*

What did that mean? There was no answer she could give. The thought fluttered away like sand in the wind.

Chapter 2

*Jerusalem
The Festival of Pesach*

The city was awash with throngs of people who had travelled from near and far to celebrate the Passover with all its various rules and regulations. Followers of Judaism would endeavour to make the sacred journey at least once in their lives. Yeshua had undertaken it several times and, even at his young age, had established a formidable reputation with his scriptural knowledge and his astonishing debating skills. He gave many a rabbi severe cause for further thought, examination, or interpretation.

This festival was of heightened interest for an exciting reason, one that was indeed rare. News had spread of the arrival of a Prince Ravanna of Orissa from the southern area of India. He had with him a retinue of Brahmin priests. His reputation had preceded him. It was said he was a fair and just ruler with a reputation for tolerance and a passion for learning. His reason for visiting Jerusalem was to learn of the wisdom the West had to offer.

THE MAGDALENE MISSION

The prince was dressed in lightweight bright-red robes brocaded with gold and silver. He was tall and dark, with a mane of lush black hair tied back in a knot that was decorated with blue and gold brocade. His skin was smooth and brown, and his large, intense, equally brown eyes highlighted his intelligent face. He received a warm welcome from the rabbis and Chief Rabbi Hillel. His curiosity and appreciation deepened still more when he was told of Yeshua. Hillel told him that Yeshua was being called 'Day Star' and he had been sent from Elah above. He was convinced that Yeshua was to bring a light to men's minds and hearts. It would not be long until he would shine as a beacon of redemptive light on the people of Judea and the whole world. Ravanna was deeply intrigued.

For several days, the prince listened and joined in with Yeshua's debating skills, wisdom, and discourses. He was astonished that a young man had such knowledge and understanding and vowed not to leave for home without taking Yeshua with him. They could learn much from each other.

Rabbi Hillel brought Yeshua to the prince and, after the formal greetings had finished, both Prince and Yeshua struck an instant rapport. Those listening could not fail to see the understanding they had between each other. Both Joseph and Mary were introduced to the prince and, with great deference, Ravanna made his request to allow Yeshua to accompany him back to India. He also explained his reasons for doing so.

Now, both parents had a secret that they had dared not tell anybody. The circumstances of Mary's conception – the angel Gabriel, and Elah's message – had been kept from their son and everybody else.

Who would ever believe them?

They were now increasingly aware that there was something extraordinary about their son. He was blessed and there was a brush of heaven around his presence. This was as it was meant to be.

With this in mind and the exceptional opportunity being offered to their son, they agreed with little hesitation. They felt much sadness at the thought of him no longer being around, but Yeshua's obvious happiness at the offer was a joy to see. The prince, to express his gratitude, presented Mary and Joseph with a floor-standing casket brim-full with Tyrian silver shekels. It was enough to last them several lifetimes.

Two days later, Yeshua said a sad and tearful farewell to his parents. After a long uneventful journey, a joyful populace welcomed Ravanna home. Yeshua was soon introduced and widely acclaimed. After several rituals, he was accepted into the Brahmin temple of Jagannath. Here, he began his learning and education in the written Sanskrit Law of Manu, the Manu-Smriti from the Vedas and Dharmashastra. His tutors were amazed at his grasp and how he was so easily able to interpret the deepest, almost mystical, meanings contained within.

For the young Yeshua, a very long term of instruction, elucidation, and education had just begun.

His heart and mind rejoiced. This was, he knew, his birthright. He never doubted it. This was what he had been born for.

Chapter 3

Magdala
Three Years Later

The waters of Galilee's sea continued their endless motion, depositing on and cleansing the ever-receptive shoreline. The light was fading, and the fishermen were beginning their nightly fish and nets were being prepared for the evening's catch. There was much heaving and groaning plus the creak of weary wet timbers.

Watching them and standing as a statue, the Magdalene. How long she had been there she knew not. The sun was dipping beyond the horizon and its reflection cast a tumultuous dark whisper of an orange disc upon the calm waters.

Her mind gave her little comfort. There were many issues that were now troubling her. She had often thought of Yeshua and the last time she had seen him on that hilly track. When she did, it was as if it were but yesterday. Since that time, she had learnt of his departure to India and whilst pleased for him, she experienced a sense of loss. At that time, she had not understood, but she now comprehended those few words he had spoken to her. Nobody she knew of, even the rabbis, had gotten as close.

He was like nobody else she had ever seen or heard. Her most secret wish was to be beside him and until her dying day.

When he was gone, her recurring dreams had vanished, and it was only of late that they had begun reappearing. The images and whisperings were as before but she sensed some clarity stirring in them. Mentioning it to her parents on several occasions had only brought their dismissal of her as childish and they had told her she would soon grow out of them. Her brother Lazarus and her sister Martha told her she lived too much inside her head and if she weren't careful, devils would take her as their own. This was a charge she had heard many times about her solitariness and frequent silences.

That evening, after the family had eaten, another of her concerns surfaced.

Joshua, her father, told her, "Mary, I spoke to Daniel earlier today and he has asked for you to be his wife. He is a fine man, Mary, and your mother, Ruth, was thrilled. He has a thriving food business and many goats, sheep, and even cattle. He said he had taken a liking to you. You would both produce fine children. Of that I am certain. I would like to tell him yes and we could arrange a marriage date. We are happy for you. It is a rare opportunity. This time can I tell him it's to be? He's different from the others and the best yet."

Mary felt as if she was being marched into an animal cage such as the Romans kept their beasts in. Her heart went heavy, and a deep sigh emitted from her. She had, much to her parents' shame and disquiet, rejected two former suitors, Adam the carpenter and Fishel the weaver.

THE MAGDALENE MISSION

"Father, I do not wish to be married and I will not! I do not even like the man. When I marry, not that I wish to, it will be of my own choosing, not anybody else's." She raised her voice and turned her back on her parents.

"Woman, you are mad," roared her father. "What people say about you is true. You must be possessed by the seven demons. No man is going to want you when they hear this about you."

"You're a woman." Her mother added her shout. "You are to have children. That's why God gave you a womb and breasts and you are forsaking his blessed gift. You bring shame on yourself, and on our name. Joshua is right, you are possessed by demons. They have taken you over! Look at yourself. You barely speak or join in with anything. You have had three marriage proposals that any woman in Magdala would have been proud to receive. All you want to talk about are your stupid dreams and that no-good Yeshua. We never met, and I heard he had left Judaea. Get much older, Mary, and no man will want you. Mary, you are truly mad, and something must be done to bring you back into the real world. The demons need to be driven from you! Hear my words loud and clear!"

The Magdalene clenched her fists and her voice rose. "I hear you both and I've no wish to be married. I have no desire in my heart and surely that's where love must come from? For me it cannot be any other way. I will not!"

Storming from the house, she ran back to the shoreline where, with a sharp gasp, ignoring its dampness, she sat heavily on the sand. Watching the gentle ripple of the sea's placid waters for some time allowed her anger to ripple away, subside. As it slid away from her an inexplicable silence entered her mind. Totally alone, she became aware of a deep peace pervading her entire being. Thoughts dropped away from her.

All still.

Whisperings.

Mary could hear them, clear and lucid, more than ever before, as if the sea was calling her.

Magdalene, Magdalene, Magdalene, peace be with you listen well. Your time is upon you. Make haste. Be not afraid. He awaits you and you alone will find him.

The words repeated and repeated and, as they did, they gradually began to fade as waves dying upon the shore but leaving her with profound certainty and peace. There was no doubt. It was Yeshua calling her. She had never forgotten his words... *You alone will find me.* It was him reaching out for her and there could only be one response she could offer. With her mind, and whispered words, she let her thoughts blow across the sea. "I shall find you, no matter how long it takes. We have not forgotten each other. I shall start soon. Guide me if you can. I've waited for this for so long,"

Her heart sang and her spirit rose like a soaring eagle.

It was with a heavy heart and a mixture of conflicting emotions that, two days later, she departed. Nobody in her family, or anyone else, had been told. To do so would have caused an unimaginable uproar and forcible confinement would have resulted. They would have her declared insane.

She had taken what she needed in terms of clothes and personal items in a small bundle on her back, plus her kinnor, and said she was off to wash all her things in the nearby canal that led directly into the old port area. She had money enough to sail to India, but where she went from there, she had no idea.

For her, for him, it had begun.

Chapter 4

*City of Prague, Czech Republic
Novotel Praha Hotel, Wenceslas Square
The Present Day*

Matthew G. Croxley, an American citizen, sat drinking a cappuccino from a bowl-sized cup and staring out across the famous square, watching the endless traffic and countless throngs of people passing by. The scene was dominated by the mounted figure of Saint Wenceslas brandishing his pennant. Croxley, at sixty-two years of age, retained a surprising youthfulness enhanced by the fashionable cut of his light-blue suit and matching button-down shirt. He was not tall, but four inches under six foot, and his tanned, shaven head gave him a pugilistic air. Hard, but small, grey eyes sat close together beneath black eyebrows.

Croxley was a man on a mission.

The venue had been well chosen. It was a country predominately indifferent to religion. He was a TV Evangelist, leader of the God's Chosen Evangelist Church. The media and other Christians frequently decried it as fascism dressed in religious clothing. He was scornful and dismissive of such accusations. He had God's approval, did he not? A world-wide following gave testimony to his claim to be personally in touch with The Almighty. He didn't doubt that the Czech Republic, like most countries worldwide, was brim-full of heretics, apostates, atheists, and other sinners of all degrees. For him and his followers, there were far too many people attempting to devalue the Bible, God's Holy Commandments, and the authenticity of Christ himself. It had to be stopped by whatever means necessary, and that meant *any* means He didn't doubt for one moment that God and his son Jesus the Christ had appointed him to fulfil and lead others into holy war to restore the truth and put Satan, his followers, and their sinful works into everlasting hellfire from which there would be no escape. One of the promised joys of heaven would be to look down and watch sinners burn in eternal agony, frying and sizzling until God's end of days was pronounced. He wasn't slow to realise, even in the country he was in, that there was a potential for his brand of right-wing ultra-conservative TV Evangelism. It gained followers in whatever country it was seen.

That was not the reason he was here.

He glanced at his smartphone. His guest was due any moment. The next minute, a bright-yellow taxi with the company's name, *Hello*, clearly visible on the doors pulled up outside the hotel – his visitor had arrived. *Hallelujah, he's here on time.*

There was no mistaking him as he walked into the reception area. The receptionist pointed him in the direction of where Matthew Croxley was sitting.

He stood up and the bishop recognised him at once, raised his hand, and strode swiftly towards Croxley, causing a draught of air-conditioned coolness in the wake of his black cassock billowing around him.

Bishop Ignatius was a portly figure, but his cassock, encircled with a gold and green band cincture, disguised his mass. His amaranth-coloured zucchetto held firm to his head. Around his neck, down to his waist, hung a large silver crucifix. Affixed to his left wrist with a thick, stout chain was a fat brown travel case.

Croxley saw a man of devotion, and set into his florid, well-fed, fleshy face were the hardest pair of iron-like eyes he had yet to encounter. At first glance, he knew he had chosen wisely. Both of them, he was certain from their preliminary discussions via Skype, were on the same path and had the same intent. There was the possibility they could work together, in spite of their differences. What was important was that their objectives were in harmony.

Ignatius inclined his head towards Croxley and made the sign of the cross.

Croxley, not comfortable with Catholic religious rituals, and feeling mildly embarrassed, responded with a slight bow as they shook hands. Cordial greetings and polite preliminary chat ensued before their main reason for meeting was opened up. The chained case lay flat on the table.

Ignatius was a Jesuit from Caracas, Venezuela. He was trilingual, with a good working knowledge of many languages. With Pontifical approval, he headed up 'DISH,' otherwise known as the 'Department for the Investigation of Suspected Heresies,' and other fake items, many claiming to be related to the Dead Sea Scrolls. It was comprised of a team of esteemed Catholic academics, research experts, and scholars whose intent was to preserve the 'one true faith' and destroy anything that was in contradiction to Biblical truths.

To a man, they loathed anything to do with the Dead Sea Scrolls and wished they had never been discovered.

Ignatius wiped a dribble of coffee from his double chin. "Matthew, it is right that we meet here in this God-forsaken city. It gives us some neutral ground to stand on. We may be on different sides of a theological fence, but the good Lord has given us grace in which we can activate his wishes. You have heard the latest from the media on this so-called 'Magdalene Mission.' It is nothing short of an attack on God's Bible, its sacred truths, and his Beloved Son Jesus Christ himself. It is outrageous and must be stopped at all costs. You do agree, don't you?" Ignatius's cheek twitched several times with a noticeable flutter of rage.

Croxley liked what he was hearing. "Of course, Bishop. It is an attack on God's Holy Word. I blame those 'Dead Sea Scrolls' and that scurrilous Dan Brown film *The Da Vinci Code*. Those phony and fake gnostic so-called gospels like Thomas and Philip are responsible, and now this unholy fraudulent rubbish displayed in Berlin, the Gospel of Mary Magdalene, that woman of dubious morality, a ten-cent whore. I even hear there's supposed to be a gospel attributed to the blessed Christ himself. It has to be stopped!" Feeling his ire rising, and to emphasise his emotions, he brought his clenched fist down hard on the table.

Ignatius responded, "True, my friend. We are now at war with secular forces, and they must not win one battle. We have to win all, at whatever cost. That's my appointed post from our beloved pope and our Catholic faith. Unbelievers and anyone who seeks to undermine God are our enemies and have to be eradicated in his holy name. I must add, news of my mission here is not known, nor must it be known to the pope." Little flecks of spittle from his fleshy lips projected across the tabletop.

Croxley welcomed the bishop's anger. He was saying everything he wanted to hear. "Bishop, these fakes must be destroyed before they destroy us. Powerful forces oppose us. This Magdalene Mission is backed and funded by some powerful worldwide organisations. They are, I fear, formidable opponents with endless cash reserves."

"Matthew, our Christian soldiers, led by Christ himself, will not be beaten. We shall overcome and destroy them. I am tracking every move this Magdalene Mission makes. They seek to find ten missing pages from her heretical, so-called gospel. This must not happen, and if such trash is ever found it must be destroyed, never to be seen. It is nothing less than an attack on our beloved Saviour and the word of God himself." Ignatius paused to mop his brow with a large purple handkerchief. He continued. "This, Matthew, is the reason for our meeting. Our intelligence sources have monitored the situation closely and your name arose several times as a person who could possibly assist us." He stared hard at Croxley, pausing to make a pyramid of his fingers upon the table, causing the chain to rattle.

With a quizzical expression, Croxley raised an eyebrow. "How can that be, Bishop?" He smelt the aroma of rewarding possibilities.

"What I am about to say may not be to your liking but hear me out to the end. We think you are the ideal person to put a stop to this proposed search. The reason this is so, is that 'Matthew Croxley' is not your real name, is it? It's Scott Hilton, and you are an ex-offender, having spent seven years in prison for robbery, fraud, and assault. You also have a master's degree in theology you obtained whilst in prison. Once released, you – it seems – had a talent for persuading people to your uncompromising viewpoint on the way Christianity should be steered. You made much money from it. Lo and behold, you changed your name and identity, and God's Chosen Evangelical Church was born. We also know that you have a way of dealing with any dissenters or objectors at any of your rallies. We have seen the video evidence and it is not gentle, but effective. This, we concluded, might be a way of preventing this evil research from proceeding further. The Catholic Church cannot be involved in any such actions and what they might entail. We have considered everything, and from what we have heard and seen, our objectives in this matter are the same. We are prepared to fund whatever actions are required to bring this project to a halt. You have been patient and have not interrupted, so please speak now." Ignatius leant back in his chair and took a deep breath. He had never before had to perform a tricky task such as this and didn't quite know what response he was going to get.

Croxley said nothing but returned a long, hardened gaze at the bishop. Absentmindedly, his fingers strayed to twirl the lapel badge he was wearing. It depicted the flag of his church. It was bloodred with a prominent white circle on which was superimposed a thick black crucifix, and not so different from the Nazi flag.

Neither man spoke.

Croxley was the first to break the silence. "You boys have been busy, haven't you? How the hell did you discover all that? I am impressed. Yep, it's true, I don't deny it." He leant forward and looked both left and right. "I like the idea. At the right price, it could be arranged. I can guarantee I have the means at my disposal."

The bishop tapped the case he was chained to. He then

delved into part of his cassock and produced a key. He held it up for Matthew to see. "In this case, Matthew, are a million Euro bearer bonds drawn on the IOR – the Institute for Religious Works, otherwise known as the Vatican Bank. If you accept this assignment, these funds will be paid into your account on a regular, automatic payment system, for a total of a million Euros. When the work is completed, there could be an extra bonus, which we can discuss at a later date. You will find that we can be quite generous."

Croxley's eyes gave an appreciative glow. In his mind, he had already made the conversion to dollars. "Show me."

The bishop inserted the key and unlocked the case to reveal a precise and beautifully arranged display of bonds, exactly as he had said. He allowed a long and intent gaze before snapping the lid tightly shut.

Croxley wasn't going to give an immediate reply. It was best to be seen thinking it over and the longer the better. It was the bishop who wanted to organise a hit of some sort on a suspected research team and, even better, to destroy anything found. In principle he agreed with him. Anything discovered would only compound the difficulties all Christian churches worldwide had with Gnostic so-called gospels. Like the bishop had said, there were only four canonical gospels, anything else was heresy. Perpetrators of such material should be punished and forced to retract, and if that meant the use of violence, so be it.

"Is there a problem?" Ignatius asked, not being used to delayed replies.

"Nothing immediate. Before I make a decision, I presume you have files on the project, like names, locations, funding, etcetera. Also, where and when to start? Without this I couldn't even begin."

"Matthew, not for one moment would we expect you not to have full information. On your acceptance, the contents of this case will – by large, regular instalments – be paid into your chosen account. You will be given full information and complete character profiles and particulars of those involved. My department has been most thorough, and you will find all intended locations, dates, and a host of ancillary information on what they hope to find and what it means to our church, and of course yours. All we ask of you is a weekly progress report. Upon successful completion, the remaining balance of Euros will be deposited into your chosen bank account. This Magdalene fairy tale must be consigned to the incinerator of history where it truly belongs."

Croxley said nothing but adopted a serious look of consideration. Eventually he spoke, but still refrained from accepting the offer enticingly displayed to him across the table. "Not an unattractive offer, Bishop, and well within our organisation's capabilities. You mentioned the possibility of bonuses. What might they be?"

"A successful mission would be the destruction of any material that's found and relating to this matter. That would warrant at least another quarter of a million. An attractive offer, I'm sure you will agree." Ignatius gave an ingratiating smile.

This time there was no hesitation from Croxley. With one hand, he gave the case a sharp slap and closed the lid. He then grasped the bishop's clammy hand and shook it. The deal was done.

Chapter 5

The Egyptology Department
The National Museum of Berlin
Bodestraße 1-3, 10178 Berlin, Germany

Professor Isabella Vanton's blonde ponytail appeared to twitch as she lifted her head higher to bring her varifocal glasses into focus. Her objective appeared in view. It was one that she and her small team had been given unlimited access to. Given the heavyweight backing of the Smithsonian Institute, the British Library, the British Museum, and the Israel Museum of Jerusalem, the way had been easily paved for some serious research. Known as the Berlin Codex, what remained of the Gospel of Mary was laid out for her to view. Though it was not classed as a canonical work, there were those she knew who refuted it as a 'gospel.' Nevertheless, there were also many adherents who said that didn't matter. It was a papyrus that had been dated to the 5th century, or even earlier, and was written in the Sahidic Coptic language. It first came to light in 1896, having been purchased in Cairo by a keen-eyed German diplomat. Since that time, it had been the subject of considerable interest and controversy and remained the subject of numerous religious debates. There were those who condemned it as some sort of elaborate fake. Others regarded it as genuine and almost mystical in its content.

Isabella was not so sure what to think, and she was not alone. The academic world, since the discovery in 1945 of the Dead Sea Scrolls at Nag Hammadi, and the new wave of contemporary scholars, had come to a corporate agreement to investigate Mary's gospel in depth. There were ten missing pages, and there was no answer as to why they would have been removed. There was a small chance that they were hidden somewhere, and that was the primary directive of her research. Backed by the most prestigious institutions, it was a no-expense-spared operation. If successful, the outcome would have a major impact on the current mode of religious thinking.

As a professor of religious and philosophical studies at SOAS, part of London University, her books and TV appearances had made her the perfect choice to head the project. At thirty-six years of age, she had managed to stay single, although she was never short of male companions. Born in New Delhi, India, her father was in the diplomatic corps before the family returned home to the UK when she was eleven years old. Her life was an academic one and she had wanted no other. Her upbringing in India had developed in her a deep interest in comparative religions. Later in life, when studying Gnostic texts and writings, she had arrived at the conclusion, after reading the gospels of Philip, Thomas, and Mary Magdalene, that there was an uncanny resemblance between them all. She had found herself acknowledging from her comparative studies a strong similarity between Oriental, Middle Eastern, and Western writings. That prompted her to wonder if there was any truth in the idea that Jesus had lived in India. The research certainly had a strong flavour about it. The missing pages from the codex, if found, could throw light on the theory.

Walking alongside her and part of her chosen team of four was Max. Dr Maxwell Franklin lectured at London University and was a language expert in Pali, Sanskrit, ancient Coptic dialects, and Greek, ancient and modern. Japanese was another of his working skills. He had also spent some time studying at Leh University in Ladakh, in the Kashmir region of India. Adding to this, he was an experienced hand at excavations in the Middle East. He too was fascinated by the objective of the research. Exploring the possibility that there existed a link between ancient Indian religious teachings and Western versions was a dream come true. He had a few theories of his own but kept them to himself until proof could be found.

Max had known Isabella – or Bella, as he called her – for many years. He was five years her senior and they had studied together both at Oxford and London. He had always said to himself – and to *no* other person – that if he were to marry, it would be to Bella, but nothing romantic had ever really blossomed between them. The closest that had ever happened was a quick kiss under the Christmas mistletoe.

She had told him once that he wasn't good looking but had an interesting face that she found likeable. That comment had forever stayed with him, but he never felt able to develop it. He had decided that he was married to his work and that was his wife and besides, it never argued back with him.

He was an avid archer and had only just missed Olympic selection. Apart from cooking, it was the only other thing in life he enjoyed.

KEN FRY

The curator – Herr Karl Reinhardt, a bespectacled ageing academic – gestured at the codex that was spread before them under glass to examine. "Take as long as you wish, and I know you, as experts, understand the rules and procedures when examining such items. As long as your hands are clean and dry there's no need for white gloves. As you may know, they reduce dexterity and are more likely to cause damage. I'll give you a few hours. If you have any questions, feel free to ask."

"That should be enough to start with, Karl, and thank you," Max replied with a nod and a reassuring smile.

The professor also gave her thanks and turned to Max. "I'm feeling excited. I've always wanted to see this."

"Me too. Let's start our examination and photographs."

THE MAGDALENE MISSION

"This looks so old." Max began reading what he could of the text, but he already had a translation of it from a number of secondary sources. The Codex was bound in wooden boards with leather that modern forensic examination and DNA extraction had determined as goatskin. It had been dressed in alum to soften and bleach it.

"It's the first two sections we are interested in." Isabella, as always when dealing head-on with primary sources, felt her heart quicken with anticipatory excitement. "I never fail to marvel at such ancient material. For its age, it's well preserved, although what we are looking at is a Coptic translation of the earlier Greek or original. That would have been in Aramaic, I suspect, but nobody knows. The Codex is not the original and, as I look, I can see that there were nineteen pages, and what we are looking at is incomplete. It shows clearly that pages one to six and pages eleven to fourteen are missing. There are scholars who suggest that the missing pages must even have been the original and could have been scribed by the Magdalene herself, or somebody close to her. If so, that would be sensational."

"Finding them is our objective, and if we do, I wonder what could be written on them and why were they removed?" Max bent as close as he could with his camera. "What can be made of it is that it has some uniformity. Each page has twenty-one to twenty-four lines of written text."

Isabella made copious notes to which she added her own personal thoughts and reactions. The hours passed quickly and then with precise Teutonic punctuality Reinhardt appeared, rattling a large bunch of keys. They had noted all the information they could. They both thanked him in German and told him it was possible they might need to make further visits but would let him know first.

"Danke mein Herr. Es ist möglich, dass wir möglicherweise erneut besuchen müssen, aber wissen Sie."

They then left.

"We need to talk." Her speech was as quick as the speed she walked. "Let's grab a beer or two. I've had several ideas."

"Me too," Max gasped as he struggled to keep up with her 116-paces-to-the-minute quick march from the building.

Her destination was Kilkenny's Irish pub. It was located a short distance from the museum, and it had a flavour she felt at home with. They proceeded to cross the Straße and a few strides separated her from Max. She failed to hear or see the pick-up truck careering towards her at high speed.

Max did, and without a second thought grabbed her from behind and hauled her back as she let out a loud scream.

The truck, moving at high speed, emitted a mighty roar and missed her by inches. Such was the velocity of the vehicle that she fell to the ground and lost a shoe, which went spinning in the air to land on the other side of the road.

"Holy Mothers!" Max roared. "That must have been deliberate. There are no other vehicles around." He hauled a white-faced Bella to her feet, minus one shoe.

"Oh my God, Max, you saved my life. How could he not have seen us?"

"I've no idea. C'mon, let's get your shoe and get to Kilkenny's. We've some serious issues to cover."

Bella struggled with her shoe, but it was intact.

The long bar frontage quickly came into sight, and they grabbed an outside table shielded with a parasol. It was not long before a Guinness and a German Lager were served. Thoughts of the truck were quickly forgotten.

Max spoke first. "It was interesting, but I don't think I learnt anything new, given what I've read before. What do you think?"

"I agree, but seeing it first-hand gave the whole mission a spark, and from that perspective it was very necessary. We have much to consider, and I'm thinking we will have to go to the Middle East and beyond if we are to get a good grip on this. There's been too much speculative, unsubstantiated material flying around. Whether Mary Magdalene composed the original document herself, we can only theorize."

Max interjected, "It seems true that Mary is believed to have come from Magdala on the western shore of the Sea of Galilee and was the first human being to witness the resurrected Christ – That is if he did die. More specifically, when reading Philip or Thomas and her own work, it can be easily inferred that Jesus initiated her into Eastern mystical teachings and the knowledge that everything in the universe ultimately returns to its roots, the eternal source of all, the primordial One. It says so plainly in her gospel."

"I agree." Bella was warming to her favourite topic. "The opening sequence of Mary's gospel that's on display sounds more akin to a passage from the Pali Canon or a Mahayana Sutra than a Christian text. Yeshua then goes on to speak of the nature of life and the objective and ultimate reality of the universe. By detaching oneself from the physical world, he tells her, inner tranquillity can be found." A bleep on her phone distracted her flow.

"Hang on, I have a text message." She began reading and a puzzled expression was replaced by a look of consternation. Her face paled. "Oh my God." She handed her phone to Max. "Read that. Is this a joke?"

He read it aloud.

Professor, you have to be lucky all the time. I only need to be once. Did you enjoy your near miss? It made my day. God loves me.

I could be Jehoram. I could make assassins as women. They could become the source of all your woes.'

"Damn!" His exclamation was loud and astonished. "Who the hell can it be, and why? Hey, are you okay?"

Isabella was visibly shaken, and her fingers trembled. "No, Max, I'm not. Somebody is after me and I don't know why. I can tell you now, I've received several phone calls of late where the person didn't speak, and now this. They have to be related, don't you think?"

Max looked thoughtful and ran his hand through his hair. "I don't like the sound of any of it. Could it be related to our work? I've had nothing happen to me. What of our other two team members, Kristy and Jake?"

"I don't think so. If they have, nothing has been mentioned. We will have to ask them and tell them to be careful. How the hell did this lunatic get my phone number and email address? That's scary."

"I've no idea, Bella, but these days nothing is too difficult. I think we have to switch into high-alert mode. What's our next move?"

"I'll call the other two and tell them we all need to meet urgently. There's not much else we can achieve here in Berlin. I think we will have to travel farther afield."

Chapter 6

Studentisches Kulturzentrum Sconenberch
Stübbenstraße 10
10799 Berlin

Bishop Ignatius had no difficulty in arranging accommodation and worship study time for Croxley's chosen operator, Alexa Heléne. She checked in under another name and passport, Miriam James. She had no idea what name she'd been given at birth.

This Opus Dei study centre offered cultural and spiritual activities and international evenings where overseas students were made more than welcome. These opportunities were of no interest to her, but attending a few would help her covert activity, of that she was convinced. She was also convinced that, with the speed events were moving, she would not be staying long in Berlin.

Taking a deep breath, she surveyed herself in the full-length mirror. She liked what she saw.

A few inches under six feet, she was a good-looking woman with black hair. Chiselled features rested under coffee-coloured skin, which gave her a Hispanic flavour. Her eyes, compellingly hypnotic, were the brightest blue. She had no real idea of her age. She had only the one name that her rescuers had given her, Alexa.

Matthew Croxley and his God's Chosen Evangelist Church had been operating close to the Mexican border when they found her alone and abandoned. She had been dumped across the border, alone with no ID or anything recognisable that could pinpoint who she was. Extensive investigations produced nothing. The church had its own HQ with available accommodations, and she had been placed in their care, where guardian parents were appointed and took care of her. Alexa Heléne began the lengthy process of learning English.

Forever grateful to the church, there was nothing she wouldn't do for Croxley and the cause. Belief in their aims and objectives was, for her, total. She had a renowned temper, and it was said she carried weapons, and there were times she had been seen practicing with them.

Croxley always felt safe when she was close by. He carried a secret. He'd once said out aloud that he wished there was someone who could get rid of one of his contenders for leadership, the far-too-liberal Pastor Jim Roberts. It was three days later that Roberts was found dead, half submerged in the local levee. His throat had been gashed open.

She had whispered to Croxley that the job had been done.

He hadn't said a word but gave a short nod. He understood. For that, she was appointed his bodyguard.

There had been numerous assignments and not one had Alexa failed. All had been outside the law. This mission was to be her most important by far and involved nothing less than total war on the Antichrists who sought to undermine God's Son Jesus by their use of the media, books, movies, the

THE MAGDALENE MISSION

arts, science, education, and verbal debates. Her prime objective – the new initiative set up with massive funding to champion the so-called Magdalene Gospel, and the rumour that they were looking for the missing pages. There was no way that this would be allowed to occur. They had to be obstructed in every possible way and violence in all its forms was to be of major importance. If people had to be eliminated, that was God's will in action.

Sitting on the bed, she allowed an event from the last forty-eight hours to run through her mind. They had not been dull.

First, she had been sitting in a nearby bar having a quiet drink. There was a yearning to reawaken dormant skills.

"Hi, you look lonely. Mind if I join you?" *He didn't wait for an answer but pulled up a chair and sat opposite her with a confident smirk.*

She had noticed him eyeing her earlier and she knew what he was after. He needed to be encouraged. "Please do." *She gave him an alluring smile.* "My name's Alexa." *She held out her hand.*

He grasped it, holding on to it longer than necessary.

She let him and could feel his soft skin with moist sweat adhering to it.

"Hi, I'm Bruno. What are you doing here all alone?"

This ungodly creep doesn't know what he's in for. She licked her lips, long and slow. "Hoping I might have some company, and it looks as if I do now." *The effect she was having on him wasn't hard for her to see. Less than an hour later, she had accepted his inevitable offer of a coffee or two at his home.*

A short time later, at his place, she commented, "Bruno, you make excellent coffee, you are very good at it."

"Sweetheart, it's not the only thing I'm good at." *He gave her a lusty grin and moved in closer to her, placed his hand on hers, and* moved his leg against hers. He kissed her cheek.

"That was nice." Her voice had a soft purr to it. "I prefer being kissed standing up." She stood, placing herself against a wall. At the same time, she lifted her head expectantly and moved her hands behind her back.

With a look of triumph, Bruno moved in fast, barely restraining himself. His hands went to her breasts as he swiftly began unbuttoning her blouse. He failed to see her look of contempt as, from behind her denim jeans waistband, she disgorged her favourite weapon. With a swift, silent movement, the titanium surgical scalpel blade was freed. He was panting with lust and she felt him hardening against her. She reached down to his trousers and faster than a heartbeat the blade slid in. So sharp and fast he never felt it until she drew it sideways at a rapid right-angle movement.

His initial sexual pleasure ceased. He dropped to the floor in a frenzy of agony and disbelief.

Blood gushed. Skin split and ripped. Vital arteries were severed, and he was beyond help. She moved back. Her face was without expression as she tilted his screeching head back and slit his throat open all the way across.

It was over.

She walked back into the night with a deep sense of a job well done. Lustful sinners got the punishment they so rightly deserved. It had been far easier than her attempt to mow down the professor woman with a truck. There would be other times to come, and she was already enjoying it. The text she had sent the woman would no doubt have had an effect, as it was so meant to. She began devising a strategy. She had comprehensive details concerning the team that had been assembled.

There was also a sophisticated listening device hidden in the professor's rooms.

Chapter 7

Belmont Apartments
Prenzlauer Berg, Berlin
2.1 Miles from the City Centre

Both Kristy and Jake had rooms at the same address. The apartments were quiet and away from the noise of central Berlin's traffic. Their next move was to discuss what they knew so far and where and what they were to do next. They were all to meet in Professor Isabella's room and finalise their future plans.

Isabella remained nervous but had received no more silent phone calls or menacing or unknown text messages. She had resolved never to be alone when outside and requested them all to help out when she asked. There was no disagreement.

Max opened up the meeting. "We've all seen and studied what we could of the codex, so first, Kristy, what are your thoughts?"

Kristy, a bright, attractive, red-haired woman in her early thirties, had recently finished, together with Jake, a postgraduate course in ancient Middle Eastern and medieval history. "Well, we won't be finding them here in Berlin. We need to go to the source."

"Do you mean Israel?" Jake looked up eagerly. At a similar age, he was a rugged-looking man but had a completely surprising personality. He was known for his compassion and gentleness. He was, and remained, a passionate history scholar and his entire life was wrapped around it.

"It's a starting point, but Bella has some interesting thoughts too." Max gave her a sharp glance.

"Yes, I have," she replied. "What I am about to say doesn't sit too well with conventional viewpoints. I've been doing some extensive research around the lives of Magdalene and Jesus and both of them have gigantic gaps in their life stories. There are eighteen unaccounted years, roughly, for both of them, and a handful of scholars believe there's sufficient evidence that they were married and had a child or children. Their union was completed in India, and his wisdom, much of which he imparted to her, she wrote down or had someone do it for her.

"Jesus initiated her into the mystical teachings and the knowledge that everything in the universe ultimately returns to its roots, the eternal source of all, the primordial One. Several researchers have reached similar conclusions and if we follow this trail, we will be visiting India and as close to Tibet as we can get." She paused to sip her coffee.

Max interjected, "I think you're right, Bella. Tibetans, and Indians close to their border, had an eternal passion for writing everything down. They have written material up to three thousand years in age, but most has been copied through the centuries, save through deterioration, and from what other researchers have come across there's a good

THE MAGDALENE MISSION

chance we may find something as dramatic or more so than the Dead Sea Scrolls."

"Okay, Max, let me say just this. If my studies are correct, Yeshua, as his name was, did at the age of twelve and after the Passover set off to India with a certain Prince Ravanna from India, who was astonished at his understanding and knowledge. Whether the Magdalene went with him is not known, but references are made to the Gospel of Mary Magdalene being written down, along with another known as the Gospel of Issa, which, to me, is a strong alliterative version of the name Jesus or Yeshua. So let's begin and map out an overall itinerary for Israel and then on to India if, as I suspect, we will have to go farther afield."

There was an excited buzz between them all and they agreed that once in Israel they would have to visit Jerusalem and the town of Magdala.

Matthew G. Croxley listened intently to his phone. Her unmistakeable voice, as sepulchral as a cold crypt, emitted a sound as cruel and sharp as razor wire.

"I got some practice in. He was a vile, sensuous sinner. He deserved nothing less. There was a lot of blood, and it was messy. I don't know who he was, nor do I wish to. Don't worry, there's not a trace of me anywhere. The professor woman I missed by an inch, but she will have received my message. There are four of them, so I am going to have fun, am I not?"

"Enjoy doing God's work. He would not want it any other way. Follow them wherever they go on this planet."

"I installed the bug while they were out, and I heard them later say they are planning to go to Israel and then on to India. I am going to have plenty of opportunities."

"Alexa, you are doing good work. I must know if they find anything. If they do, it will more than likely be destroyed once I've seen it. You do understand that, I hope?"

She agreed. Matthew's emphasis left her in little doubt.

"Keep me informed, and I will be in touch with Bishop Ignatius to see if he knows of anything that might be of help to you in Jerusalem."

"Matthew, they are also talking of extending their trip to beyond India if they have to."

"Good. That will give you plenty of opportunity to successfully carry out your sacred mission. Never forget that God is with you for all things you have to do to put a stop to any findings."

"I have ideas and plenty of skills that they will find out to their cost."

"Well, I know, and remember. God has given you an abundance of expertise. Use it well and report back to me soon as you can. It might be better if they find something and then we can make a decision on what to do with them."

Their conversation ended and his next call was a report to Bishop Ignatius.

Chapter 8

The flight from London to Israel would take under five hours. Ben Gurion Airport at Lod was a thirty-five-minute drive from Jerusalem. They had booked in at the Hotel Villa Brown, a short journey from the city centre.

They were seated close together and began making plans for the next day's itinerary. Isabella could not shake a feeling of apprehension. The encounter in Berlin and the text message had caused her to be jumpy about any strangers or being alone. She made certain that Max was close by at all times. Kristy and Jake had been told and all four of them were now on alert as much as possible.

Four seats away from them, a woman with a tanned complexion and vivid blue eyes never let them from her sight. She could hear what was being spoken.

It was decided that they would operate in pairs. Two would find what they could in the Holy City. The other two would go on to Magdala and see what they could source from the area.

Isabella spoke. "I don't think there's much we can find in

either location. Excavations and digs have left no stone unturned. But we must keep on trying. I have a few other thoughts. The Temple of the Mount was the HQ of the Knights Templar, and their patron saint was Saint Mary Magdalene."

"What are you suggesting?" Jake had become wide awake. "Are you saying there could be a link here?"

"I just don't know, but they were extremely devoted to her. When you think of the other choices they could have made, they chose a woman whom the Catholic Church had, until recently, branded across the centuries as what we call today a sex worker. There had to be a reason for that."

"Not difficult." Max offered a good reason. "The gospels of Thomas and Philip make no mention of miracles or divine transformations, nor does the Gospel of Mary. According to them, she was Christ's favoured one and that her understanding of his words far outstripped that of his disciples."

Kristy, not wanting to be left out, offered her opinion. "Whether we find these pages or not, I think we're going to learn more than we already know right now."

"A small consolation that would turn out to be, wouldn't it? There has to be something out there that can help us unravel this mystery." As Jake spoke, he looked uncomfortable. The woman with bright-blue eyes was staring hard at him. When she noticed him looking, she smiled at him, revealing a perfect row of bright-white teeth before turning to gaze out of the cabin window. Shrugging, he thought no more of it and dismissed it as just another person being friendly.

Max looked thoughtful. "What I am hoping for is that somewhere out there, we can find some evidence or a strong possibility that the India connection can be made, and it can

THE MAGDALENE MISSION

link in with Jerusalem and her gospel. I hope your India theory can be proven correct, and if it bears out, we can really begin to track the missing pieces of this puzzle."

"Well, we have as long as it takes, and the world is our oyster in which we hope to find a pearl." Bella held his arm. "I just want no more speeding cars or trucks coming too close. I'm still shaky from that and that message. I've racked my brains trying to work out who it could have been, but I have no idea."

He gave her hand a squeeze. "Forget it. Just some crazed loon and, anyway, we are far from Berlin now. There will be no more of it."

The blue-eyed woman could hear every word and gave a sardonic smile. *Wishful thinking, I fear.*

The hours passed for what was an uneventful flight. Once landed, they proceeded through the usual airport checks. There was an obvious abundance of armed police and military to hand and, given the state of Middle Eastern politics, it wasn't surprising. Less than an hour later, they checked in at the Villa Brown, a warm and friendly hotel with a raft of amenities, which included a work desk in every room. There were also fine-dining and bar areas. They agreed to meet later in the bar.

Later that evening, Jake was the first one there and he sat himself at a bar stool while waiting for the others to arrive. It was then that he saw her sitting at a table in a corner. Gazing at him was the same blue-eyed woman who had smiled at him on the plane. He gave a start and quickly looked away.

Without knowing why, the previous feeling of being uncomfortable returned and he had no reason for it, nor was he able to understand it. At that moment, his three companions appeared. Isabella carried a large folder and several maps. He turned to see if he was still being stared at, but the woman had vanished.

"Hey, Jake, you okay? You look worried," Max remarked.

"I'm okay, thanks, but there was a woman on our plane who kept staring at me. Now, unbelievably, she was sitting just over there a minute ago and was staring at me again. I find it unnerving and stretching coincidence a bit too far."

Max laughed. "Lucky you, Jake. Looks like your handsome face is having an effect."

Isabella frowned. "Let's hope it is a coincidence. After my episode, things like that are unsettling and worrying. Let's forget it for now. Should it happen again, we'd know it's more than just a coincidence. Kristy and Jake, I have here a street map of Magdala and several of Jerusalem. I suggest that when you arrive tomorrow, visit the archaeological dig site. Your credentials and accreditations will give you unlimited access. They have uncovered a first-century town and the alleged home of the Magdalene. That should give you an appetite to look further. Also, there's the Magdala Stone with ancient carvings, and it has the oldest-known seven-branched menorah inscribed on it. While you're there, visit the Migdal Synagogue. It is fascinating to think she and Yeshua could have once been in the very same place you may be standing on. Take photographs and make notes. Max and I will go to the Holy Mount and surrounding area to see what we can find. I think you will have more fun than we will. C'mon, let's have a few more drinks and then off to bed."

THE MAGDALENE MISSION

It moved with silent stealth, unseen and in no hurry. Its tongue, tasting the air, flicked around and in and out of its huge half-open mouth. The black mamba rippled across the top of the twenty-foot curtain rail before commencing its imperceptible slither down the hidden side of the drapes.

Kristy was standing looking out of the window across the twinkling lights of the ancient city. She was feeling sleepy, and it had been a long, hard day, and there was a lot to get through the following day. Jake was in the adjoining room, as had been agreed. It was time to get into her bed with its enticing crisp white Egyptian cotton sheets. She began to peel off her clothes. For modesty, she commenced pulling the curtains together with a handful of vigorous tugs.

She saw it.

At first, she did not believe what she was seeing. Then she did as it turned to slide away and let out a loud hiss. For a split second she froze before her mouth opened wide and she screamed in fear.

The adjoining door burst open, and Jake rushed in. "What's going on?" he shouted at her.

One hand covered her face and the other pointed at the snake that was now rearing up and opening its mouth.

Jake seized her arm and dragged her away at speed before it could strike. With the other hand, he grabbed a thick duvet cover and flung it over the snake before it did anything else. The thing was entangled in the thick folds of the bedding. Moving quickly, Jake wrapped the blanket tightly around its head and most of its body before it could wriggle out or strike. Opening the window, he flung the bundle into the garden below, pushing her into his room and rushing out to find the manager and the security people.

Some minutes later, he returned to find Kristy looking shocked and shaken.

"How the hell did that thing get in here? The security guards couldn't find it, but a warning has been given to all staff and customers. The manager said it has never happened before. I must tell Bella and Max."

"Don't leave me on my own, Jake. Stay with me and we can talk about it in the morning."

"Okay, but first, I'll check both rooms, including the cupboards." Jake picked up another spare cover and proceeded to search everywhere, doing it very slowly. He found nothing. It was then that his smartphone chimed. It was a text message with a laughing emoji.

What fun 'Hissing Sid' was. Didn't you think so? He tells me 'fangs' are going to change around you. Sleep well. Bighty bite!

Jake did a double take at the mocking message. "Jesus H Christ! Kristy, look at what just came through on my phone."

She read it through. "Oh my God!" The colour drained from her face. "Isabella's assailant! It must be. We're definitely being stalked. What are we going to do?"

"I don't know. We must tell her in the morning. It may even change our plans."

The following morning at breakfast, they related the incident to Max and the professor.

There was a shocked silence.

Max broke it. "The text messages confirm it. How did they

get our addresses? Somebody knows about what our mission is. They are out to stop us. Why would that be?"

"Fanatical religious bigots are the only idea I can think of." Bella's expression hardened. "My mind is focussed on our objective and these creeps are not going to deter me. I'll take my chances and my heart and mind are truly set on achieving some measure of success. It's the chance of a lifetime. If you wish to jump ship, you are free to do so. What do you say?" She looked around at them all.

There was a momentary pause, and then it was high fives all around.

"Thank you, everyone." She looked emotional. "That's settled. We have a work programme for today, so let's get to it and meet up here later this evening. But at all costs, be alert and vigilant."

Chapter 9

A glow of satisfaction crossed Alexa's face. Her plans were working well, and she related the episodes to Croxley. She could hear his pleasure in his voice.

"Give me a little time and I will join you. I think two can operate more effectively when working in harmony. Continue with the scare tactics and they may just abandon their project. Don't eliminate them yet. That's a decision I wish to consider more deeply."

"I understand, Matthew, but—"

He interrupted her. "No buts about it, Alexa. I'd rather they find what they are looking for and then, in God's name, once read through, we can destroy it – together with them, if needs be, rather than them living to tell the world. Bishop Ignatius, with the secret blessing of his faith and bishops, has already informed me in no uncertain terms that looks to be the best course of action. Besides, we don't want the likes of these godless museums sending another team looking. The last thing we need is a display like that heretical and sacrilegious Berlin Codex. Do you understand?"

THE MAGDALENE MISSION

She rushed her reply. "I understand, Matthew. I will always abide by your wisdom and God-given words. You saved me from Hell and have given me Heaven. I enjoy the work you delegate to me and know it is given to you by God. Forgive me if I've done wrong, and I cry out for a blessing."

Croxley felt his chest expand and the sacredness of his mission overwhelmed him almost to tears. Alexa was his disciple and, through him, she was also God's. "You have my blessing, and you know it is from God himself, who has chosen us to fulfil his sacred work."

"I thank you, Matthew, with all my heart and soul, and God as my witness, I shall continue as you suggest. I have some other ideas to try out and will keep you informed of events and any discoveries." She powered down her phone and kissed her buttonhole enamel badge with its red, white, and black crucifix insignia. *Alleluia*!

Bella and Max had moved cautiously around the city, which, as ever, was thronging with countless visitors. All seemed to be on religious quests of their own choosing.

"It hasn't changed one bit since I was last here." She looked disappointed.

"The political atmosphere is as toxic as ever. It never changes," Max added. "We've also visited most holy places and apart from the Templar conundrum, hidden treasure, mysterious cargo transportations, and artefacts, nothing I can see has moved us any closer to finding anything useful."

"You are right, Max. I somehow don't think there's anything here we can latch onto. There's more to discover. I wonder how the other two are getting on?"

"Let's hope they have done better than us. A clue or something to investigate further would be most helpful."

"Max, I've continued researching and I think India is hot on the list. I dug up all sorts of material, including a BBC documentary, purporting that there was proof positive that Jesus was a Buddhist monk and allegations that he did get married."

"Can't see any church swallowing that story."

"If he did, then the allegations of marriage must be to the Magdalene. There could be no other. This is what I've found out. The story goes like this.

"In the late nineteenth century, a Russian doctor named Nicolas Notovitch travelled extensively throughout India, Tibet, and Afghanistan. He detailed his experiences and discoveries in his 1894 book *The Unknown Life of Christ*. At one point during his voyage, in 1887, Notovitch broke his leg and recuperated at a Tibetan monastery in the city of Leh, at the very top of India. It was here that monks showed Notovitch two large, yellowed volumes of a document written in Tibetan, entitled *The Life of Saint Issa*. During his time at the monastery of Hemis, Notovitch translated the document, which tells the true story of a child named Jesus, i.e., Issa, meaning 'Son of God,' born in the first century to a poor family from Israel. Jesus was referred to as the 'Son of God' by the Vedic scholars. They practised the ancient Aryan religion before Hinduism took over. Issa was schooled in the sacred Buddhist texts from the age of thirteen to twenty-nine. Notovitch translated two hundred of the two hundred twenty-four verses from the document. I think the missing ten pages complete the total number of verses.

"While Notovitch was at the monastery, one lama

THE MAGDALENE MISSION

explained to him the full scope and extreme level of enlightenment Jesus had reached. He said that Issa was a great prophet, one of the first after the past twenty-two Buddhas. He went on to tell Notovitch he was greater than any one of all the Dalai Lamas. His name and his acts were recorded in their sacred writings. He said, 'We learnt of his astounding existence in the midst of a society of ignorant and deluded people back in his native land. We at the monastery still weep at the murderous sin of his people who, not just satisfied in torturing him, attempted to put him to death in a most evil manner.'"

"So… what you're saying, Bella, is that both his and the Magdalene's missing years have been recorded in a remote Buddhist monastery in India or Tibet? That there's a record of a gospel, if you like, of Saint Issa or Yeshua? It's hard to believe."

"There's more, Max. The lama who headed the Hemis monastery also confirmed the story. The verses have since been documented by others, including Russian philosopher and scientist Nicholas Roerich who, in 1952, recorded accounts of Jesus's time at the monastery. Apparently, Issa passed his time in several ancient cities of India such as Benares and Varanasi. It was said that everyone loved him because Issa dwelt in peace with all ranks of what we call the Indian social caste system. He instructed and helped all, irrespective of their social rank. Quite how Roerich reached that conclusion is not stated, but it seems more probable than not.

"Jesus spent some time teaching in the ancient holy cities of Jagannath, Benares, and Rajagriha, which, due to doctrinal differences, provoked the Brahmins to excommunicate him, compelling him to leave for the Himalayas where he spent another six years studying Buddhism. So, everything was not so kind and peaceful as we are being led to believe. Another German scholar wrote, 'The young Jesus arrived in a region of the Sindh along the river Indus in the company of merchants. He settled among the Aryans with the intention of perfecting himself and learning from the laws of the great Buddha. He travelled extensively through the land of Punjab and stayed briefly with the Jains before proceeding to Jagannath.' Somewhere in the middle of all this, Max, the Magdalene appears. What Issa said and did was written down either by her or another, and from what I'm guessing, we will find that her words will match those of this Gospel of Saint Issa. If so, then we will have a good idea of what they mean. But where the missing pages are is still a mystery, and why have they vanished?

"In the BBC documentary *Jesus Was a Buddhist Monk*, scholars theorized that Jesus escaped or survived his crucifixion, and at thirty years of age he returned to the land he loved so much. That's not our concern. We are looking for written evidence regarding the missing pages. So, Max, what do *you* think we should do?"

Max looked thoughtful, then ran his hand through his thick hair. "Wow, that's some story, and maybe that's all it is, a fanciful tale. However, it is compelling, and it seems as if we will find more in Kashmir than we can in this city. Let's talk this evening with Kristy and Jake and see what they have found out, if anything, and how they feel. Meanwhile, let's have a chilled beer or two before we get back to the hotel."

Bella agreed and they made their way to The Barrel and The Tap, an English-style pub close by. "Max, I'm still concerned about those incidents – speeding trucks, deadly snakes, and texts. Somebody is watching us in some way or

THE MAGDALENE MISSION

another and I have no idea who it can be or why."

"Nor have I, or why, and I don't think we are going to find out either. Look, this place is almost empty." He pointed to a small nearby table. Let's grab it." Within seconds, they were seated, and the beers were ordered.

Wearing a smart black beret with a headscarf and her eyes covered with heavy wraparound designer sunglasses, Alexa Heléne watched them with close intent. Her powerful mobile listening device, looking no different from a mobile phone, was switched on and its small antenna was pointed in their direction. It was recording all that was being said, which she could also hear with her earphones. She was drinking red wine. It was the only drink she ever allowed herself. She felt it was a holy act to do so and akin to communion wine. She never drank more than two or three. *I've scared all of them a wee bit, apart from the man with her. He's next. I have something in mind.* She watched him closely, his mannerisms and body language. Clearly, he was fond of the professor. That was a weakness that could be exploited. She would need to examine what they were saying. To be doubly certain, a listening device that resembled a two-way adaptor plug had been plugged into a wall socket in their room. Getting into it while they were out had not been a problem. She had been trained well.

Chapter 10

Magdala

The Sea of Galilee barely had a ripple on its surface. It was a perfectly still… a windless day. The sea was famed for its fish, and the boats were out as they had done over two thousand years back. Tourists wandered around the shoreline. Many were Christians living in hope that He would appear, walking across the waters.

Kristy and Jake were not in that brigade. They had breathed in the local atmosphere, and both said they found it beguiling. The Magdalene story had imbedded itself into the entire fabric of the place, both ancient and modern. It was inescapable.

They had made their way to the archaeological dig, eager to see what was being said of the Magdalene's house. Their credentials were accepted. There could be none better, and they were treated almost as honoured guests. The stonework was indeed ancient, thousands of years old, but with its modern interior they felt something was missing to reflect how she might have lived. To compliment this, they were

THE MAGDALENE MISSION

shown the Migal Synagogue. It was the oldest synagogue ever found in Galilee and probably the most ancient in the world.

"This place," said Jake, "must have been here when the Magdalene and Christ were alive. It is so old."

"It makes me feel humble just to look at it. It feels as if I can almost touch her."

"A lot of people say that," a strange voice spoke to them.

They swung around and found themselves facing a tall smiling man dressed in black, including a matching hat and carrying a small briefcase.

"Sorry to startle you both, but I couldn't help hearing your comments. I'm Rabbi Cohen, and I've lived here all my life. Is there any way I can help you at all?"

"No problem, Rabbi. That's very kind of you. I'm Jake and this is Kristy. We are on a major research project. Let me explain." Jake proceeded to relate the precise details of what they were looking for and the mystery surrounding the Magdalene.

Rabbi Cohen didn't say a word until the story was complete. "Let's sit for a while. I appreciate what you are trying to do. There's not much I can tell you to help you, but what I'm about to say may be of some use. As I said, I've lived here all my life, as did my family and all their generations, into the distant past. The only other place they visited, as I have myself, was Jerusalem. My lineage here in Magdala is as old as the hills that surround us. Your story is familiar to me and my family. My ancestors had been here from the time these ancient bricks were first laid. You could say the people of Magdala are, in many ways, interrelated. I feel that strongly. As a rabbi, I've made it my business to acquaint myself with Jewish religious beliefs and practices, especially compared with others. There are many similarities, and differences too. Personally, I follow the Gnostic gospels, including those of Thomas, Philip, and especially that of Mary Magdalene. Yeshua was also called Rabbi frequently and that, to me, is important. The stories my family handed down about him do mention that he disappeared for many years. It was said he left for India under the auspices of an Indian prince and some years later, she too vanished from here. He returned, together with the Magdalene, as they had become wife and husband. It was said she was the wisest and cleverest of them all and would often explain to the disciples in simple terms what Jesus said and what he meant. She wrote down much of it during her stay in India. The story is controversial, regarding them being married and him seemingly surviving crucifixion, and then they fled. No one knows where for certain, but there are many rumours – back to India, even France or England. Who knows? Does my story help you in any way?"

"I'd say it does, Rabbi." Kristy looked enthusiastic. "You have helped put flesh on bones. It looks as if we, and the rest of the team back in Jerusalem, will be heading to India very soon."

Jake nodded. "You have just confirmed everything we have been thinking and discussing. I almost think some mysterious force sent you to us. Thank you so much. We are grateful for all you have told us."

Later that evening, the team gathered around a bar table and exchanged their earlier experiences. The meeting with Rabbi Cohen gave them all cause to vote for a visit to Kashmir.

THE MAGDALENE MISSION

Isabella looked around at them all. "Often, these sorts of tales exist almost as legend and are passed from one generation to the next. It seems to add some weight to my theory and, hearing that, I am almost convinced we must make plans to get there as soon as we can."

Both Jake and Kristy agreed.

Max spoke. "That meeting was an amazing coincidence, and I wonder why that tale has not, as far as I know, been picked up by anybody. Sure, there are books about the possibility of the India story being true, but there's nothing written about the Magdalene being there at the same time. Why should we believe one lone rabbi who appears from out of nowhere and tells you exactly the story you have wanted to hear all along? I'll go along with your wishes, but my inclination is that if there's anything to be found it will be closer to home. It wouldn't surprise me, either, if those Knights Templar had a hand in it somewhere. There are too many stories about them, their secret passages, tunnels, and treasures. My main interest, as you all know, is in the close relationship that exists between various ancient religious writings of different belief systems. That's all I have to say on the subject."

"Let's not argue," Kristy interjected. "We have voted and, Max, we need you. You studied in Kashmir at Leh University in Ladakh, and we couldn't do without your expertise and knowledge of the region. Smile, be happy, and just think of what might happen if we find what we are looking for." She gave him a winning smile.

He had to laugh and gave her a quick hug. "Of course, and don't you dare go without me. Once there, we'll arrange to make our way to Hemis monastery and see where that may lead us."

It was agreed, and the following day they would begin to make preparations to take the first steps towards India. They failed to notice the woman who sat close by wearing a hijab-style headscarf and dark glasses with what looked like a mobile phone on her table pointing in their direction. Wearing earphones and dressed in a black suit, she looked no different from many women around them, similarly attired.

Alexa guessed she would be taking a trip and that required very careful planning. She could not be too obvious, or they might start getting suspicious. She needed to contact Croxley and see what ideas he had. She needed him with her. His strength would give her greater determination and courage. There were four of them and she was on her own. She allowed herself a smile, for Max was in for a little surprise.

Isabella was convinced she was going to be proved right and they would find the evidence they were looking for. Max, she understood, was non-committal and was taking a professional, academic approach to the problem. Kristy and Jake were with her in their opinions, and she was glad of that, or else she would find it tough going.

With that, they decided it was time to get to bed and they made their way to their rooms.

"Well, Bella, it looks like we're in for a lot of miles. We're going to need all the sleep we can get." Max pushed open the main door to the rooms. He paused, holding out an outstretched arm to stop her. "Stop, don't go any farther. Someone has been in here."

"Hotel staff, cleaners, etcetera. They come and go."

THE MAGDALENE MISSION

"Yes, I know, but they don't leave three sets of my clothing draped over the bed and chairs."

"I don't understand it."

"Nor do I. Look, what's that under my duvet and pillow?" He pointed to a bulky bulge in the middle of the bed. He pulled away the covers, then reeled back and shouted, "Jesus! What in God's name is that?"

Isabella shrieked loudly, covering her face with her hands. It was a dead cat and it had been slit open. Its insides were spread around the sheets. Within seconds, she was violently sick, vomiting into a hand basin.

Max gulped heavily and immediately called the management before pushing her out of the room. It was then he spotted the note pinned to the headboard. He ripped it off. It was written in a flowery cursive fashion.

Good evening, Dr. Max. Hope you enjoyed my handiwork. His nine lives have all gone. How many do you think you have left? Be careful how you go now. Repent your sins!

The manager called the police and a veterinarian to clear the mess. There was not a clue to be found. The only thing they could tell for certain was that a scalpel had been used. The police questioned Isabella and Max intensely, but nothing could be established. Kristy and Jake also co-operated but to no avail. The team knew one thing with complete certainty – they were under some sort of stalking attack. The trip to India had now become urgent and there was no way they were going to abandon it.

Chapter 11

After many hours, the Air India flight touched down at Kushok Bakula Rimpochee Airport, situated in the state of Kashmir and one of the highest airports in the world. It had not been an easy trip. Their minds were firmly ingrained with the memories of the recent episodes surrounding their quest. They had another fear that whoever was behind the attacks could also be on the flight. There was no way of knowing.

Isabella had booked them all for a one-month stay at the Hotel Tushita Ladakh. There, each room had Wi-Fi and a work desk, ideal for their notes, photographs, and translations. Max was pivotal, and language expertise was his major asset. There would be, he said, a lot of translation material to wade through. He had contacted the head lama, Gyalwang Drukpa, and explained their mission. There was no problem, and every bit of help would be made available to them on a daily basis. For their trip to Hemis and the neighbouring areas they hired a car. Max elected to drive.

"I am familiar with this region and the monastery is about an hour's drive or more from here. The distance is only forty-five kilometres. If you don't like heights, don't sit next to, or look out of the window. There are some scary drops along the road we are taking. Hemis sits at twelve thousand feet in the Subang Valley and smack-bang in the middle of the Stok Kangri mountain range. The road we will be taking is narrow and twisty. There can be no overtaking unless you have a parachute! Another thing – there are frequent rock falls and landslides, which can completely cut you off and they are often impassable. If you'd rather stay here at the hotel, you can do so. Furthermore, for your interest, the road runs alongside numerous chortens and a very lengthy prayer wall. It is full of mani. They are stones with inscribed mantras on them."

Kristy piped up, "I don't like heights, but I'm not going to be staying here on my own. Whoever that person scaring us is could also be here."

"I thought of that too." Isabella placed her arm around Kristy. "Whoever it is seems to know everything we are doing or about to do."

"We must be bugged in some way, but I've seen nothing suspicious and have searched all our clothes and luggage and haven't seen anything worrying, nor anybody on the flight. They looked like tourists and locals." Max looked thoughtful. "I suggest when we are making plans, we do so not in our rooms but in the open where bugs can't hear us."

They all agreed, and the next day they would make their first visit to the monastery.

She looked at herself in the mirror and adjusted her blonde

wig, allowing the long hair to drape over her shoulders and close to her ears, which supported her dark wraparound sunglasses. Alexa's distinctive blue eyes were now covered with grey contact lenses. Wearing her tight blue jeans, trainers, and a loose-fitting sweater with a camera over her shoulders, she looked no different from any other sightseer in the region. Her disguise was perfect and there was no chance of any of them recognising her. It was time to call her mentor, Matthew G. Croxley.

The phone was answered after six rings. She outlined events of the last few days and that they were making plans to visit Hemis.

"Alexa, by all means follow, but this time do nothing but observe and listen. Should they find what they are looking for, they will not be able to take it with them. They can only translate and photograph the material. What we need is to obtain their findings, if they have anything. They also need, somehow, to discover what happened to or who has those missing pages. Then we can strike, and strike hard we will. The bishop is anxious that any findings should never be made public, and I am of the same mind. Our faith is under attack, and we must fight by any means necessary, with every weapon at our disposal."

"Matthew, I will obey and keep in contact with you at all times. I owe you so much and you honour me with this mission."

"So be it. You are worthy. Amen." The phone went dead.

She proceeded down to the restaurant and spotted them seated together. Confident in her disguise, she found a seat close by and again made use of her listening phone device. She noted they frequently scanned the dining room. They were now obviously suspicious of everyone. She had no

THE MAGDALENE MISSION

difficulty recording every word they were saying. The machine, although small, was able to hear conversations through a wall three feet thick or more.

They had booked for a month's stay and that should give them enough time to find something and work on it in their rooms. She decided to remain at the hotel and let them rummage through records and prayers. Once their work was done, she would make her plans and hopefully meet up with her mentor, Croxley.

The following day, the sun shone as warm as ever and an air of expectation hung around them as they loaded up the car for the drive to Hemis. The search for the Tibetan scroll relating to Issa or Jesus and the Magdalene was about to begin again. They hoped that with modern knowledge and techniques they might unravel more.

The drive was precarious. Kristy sat in the middle seat with her eyes mostly closed. They climbed higher and higher on the narrow excuse for a road. The drop from the edge was on the left and the route was often down to one lane with frequent minor blockages from the mountain rocks above. To make a reversing manoeuvre as other vehicles were coming the other way was an act equivalent to a high-wire circus performer.

Terrifying.

They endured.

Crossing a bridge over a fast-flowing mountain river and through a network of tall trees seemed like a nightmare journey until the full structure of the monastery emerged into view.

Hemis Monastery | Image from India.com

Max brought the car to a halt. It was a riveting spectacle they had not envisaged. It was different from anything that they had witnessed in the West.

Isabella nodded. "Wow, there's some sort of puja going on. We'd best not interrupt it."

Monks in their colourful robes were chanting and moving around in a very wide circle.

"What's a puja?" asked Jake.

She answered, "Jake, puja is the name for ceremonies that involve offerings, or gifts. During these ceremonies, they will also meditate and offer prayers. Puja brings Buddhists to the Buddha, helping them to find answers to overcome suffering. Puja is important, as it's like a Buddhist version of Mass, but is far older."

"Okay," said Max. "When it's finished, we had better go

THE MAGDALENE MISSION

and see the head guy, Lama Gyalwang Drukpa."

An hour later, a solemn-looking junior monk ushered them into the lama's private chambers. They were uncertain of protocol but placed their palms together, bowed their heads, and used the Indian greeting *Namaste*. He greeted them in a similar fashion. He had a gentle and friendly disposition, and his English was flawless. He looked surprisingly young.

"Your group is most welcome to our humble monastery. I will show you where our records are kept. There has been a monastery of sorts here since the eleventh century. Many of our records from that time have survived. The oldest is Samyo Monastery nearby, built in the eighth century. Sadly, some of its records have not survived. Many of them are written on papyrus and on scrolls and must be handled with utmost care. As you are all skilled researchers with impressive backing and credentials, I am certain you will be faultless in your treatment of our records. Please wear your gloves. You look for the words of Saint Issa. They are somewhere in these rooms. It is a rare request, one which has only ever been asked one or two times in the past. You think Issa was your Jesus and that he lived in Kashmir for many years before he returned to his native Judea as a man with exceptional skills and wisdom, equal, many have said, to our Lord Buddha. You are all most welcome. I wish you well. You have unlimited access to our sacred relics and writings, and I look forward to hearing what you discover. Follow me."

He led him through numerous passageways and rooms before descending to a much lower level where he was confronted by two massive doors, which he flung open and strode through. It was the beginning of the library, which stretched several rooms in length and was of considerable width. The walls were covered in ancient murals and frescos depicting the life of Buddha, with racks and columns ten feet high or more and brim-full of uncountable records, scrolls, manuscripts, prayer wheels, and all manner of written material.

He explained, "The oldest stand at the far end, and each rack represents fifty to a hundred years of Buddhist writings and thought. The oldest are placed at the bottom. There's a variety of languages, whichever were in use at the time and age. These are mostly Sanskrit and Pali. Of course, there are dialects, Tibetan, and even Japanese in later versions. The wall paintings you see are not all original. Many are copies of what has been depicted in our manuscripts and scrolls, which are far older than Hemis itself. Behind you are long tables on which you may examine what you wish and, with great care, take photographs and make notes. Please remember to roll back a scroll when you have finished and replace it. The library doors will remain open for you the moment you arrive each day and locked when you leave. All our monks and others know of your presence, and all have been instructed to help you at all times if asked. If there are language difficulties, many of us here are multi-lingual and would be more than happy to assist. You may start tomorrow, and we look forward to your visit and findings." He placed his hands together and bowed low as he gave his Hindi blessing. "*Aapaka bahut-bahut svaagat hai, main aap par buddh ke aasheervaad kee kaamana karata hoon.*"

Bella smiled, and with the others, bent low. She understood. *You are most welcome. I wish Buddha's blessings upon you.*

"We are honoured and thank you deeply."

Chapter 12

Croxley had forever pursued a side hobby apart from his money-making religious-scamming actions. He had a fascination with Italian gangster films and activities. This had grown whilst in jail. To that end, he had befriended several such characters, and when he wasn't doing his sinister works himself, he would use them to that end. One went by the name Marco 'Bull' Morello. He lacked sinister cunning, but his results were no less impressive. Croxley paid well and that guaranteed his loyalty. He understood the man and his requirements, and he asked few questions.

Bull was defined by his nickname. At the age of thirteen, a group of older boys attempted to steal his skateboard in the street. His ferocity in attacking them singlehanded won the admiration of a watching group of mobsters and that was the name he was given, and thus his criminal career began. He had a deceptively lean, tall appearance, and with his dark hair and taste in Italian suits, he would not have looked out of place in a society gathering or magazine.

The almost fourteen-hour flight from JFK to New Delhi in

India was giving him cause for anxiety. Bull had two weaknesses, but neither were discernible from immediate observation. One was the thought of being confined in such an enclosed space, like a tunnel or an aeroplane. He knew his claustrophobia would kick in as soon as he stepped onto the aircraft. It would often cause him to sweat profusely, followed by a bout of sickness. The other was a fear of heights, a form of vertigo that could instigate a panic attack with just the thought of it. The idea of flying at thirty-five thousand feet coalesced both fears and he knew he would struggle. Not wishing to appear weak and silly with Croxley sitting next to him in the first-class area, before take-off, he had downed a small bottle of scotch he had brought with him. With this, he swallowed a tranquillizer, together with a sleeping pill. Croxley would be minus somebody to talk to.

In Leh, Alexa had not been idle. She arranged accommodation for both men with an open-ended booking at the hotel and would meet them on arrival at the airport. She knew Bull well and his brutal manner of going about his assignments. She had little time for his techniques. She regarded her artistic style of operating as superior in every way. Her unfelt initial thrust of a titanium scalpel was really far beyond a coshing or a bullet. It required certain skills. *Does it not?* Her surveillance of the Magdalene team was subtle and unnoticeable in any way whilst they were out and about. She watched them on their trips to and from Hemis. The next day she would search their rooms and see what they had found. Certainly at times they seemed excited. That was a clue that something could have been discovered.

THE MAGDALENE MISSION

The monks began their day very early, at five in the morning. An invitation had been given to the team, asking if they would like to join in the morning's chants and Puja. The team, who had no wish to get up much earlier to be there, politely turned down those offers.

Each of the team had their allocated tasks, as worked out with Isabella. She and Max, with their combined language skills, would work from the beginning, and Jake would start at the far end. It would be painstaking work. Kristy, bristling with cameras and her laptop, would examine the murals for clues.

"Remember," said Isabella, "we are attempting to locate Mary's gospel, or traces of it, if any are to be found. You should not be side-tracked by anything you discover about Issa, who all the monks are convinced was Yeshua or Jesus … If that's so, then we are obliged to look for any evidence or mention of her, no matter how tiny or seemingly irrelevant, so tomorrow let's get started."

As promised, all was ready for them when they returned the following day. The doors were open, and seating has been assigned. It was going to be long, tedious, and painstaking work. One month, they thought, was never going to be enough.

"I have with me," said Bella, "Notovitch's book *The Life of Saint Issa*. In it, he transcribes two hundred of the two hundred and twenty-four pages. He just couldn't have made all that up. We need to find it and those unscripted verses. With that, we might have a clue to what the missing pages of

Mary's gospel state, and even more importantly where they could be, if still in existence."

The hours went by and both Bella and Max made copious notes and took numerous photographs. Every so often there would be a tantalising reference to Issa amongst other names, but nothing else. How many more there could be, there was no way of knowing, and then there was no proof as to whom Issa might be.

It was halfway through the day when Kristy came rushing in. "Quick, you two, come with me and see what I've found. I've been photographing some of these murals to see if there could be any clues and I think I've found something remarkable."

"What's that, Kristy?"

"Wait until you see it. It needs some explanation. You might be able to throw some light on it."

They moved around a corner and Jake was busy with his camera. "There, look." He pointed to the adjacent wall. "Kristy spotted it and you have to look closely to understand it."

The other two stared hard at what seemed to be a blur of fading and ancient colours, mostly red with hints of green. "What are we supposed to be looking at?"

Kristy drew an outline with her finger.

Bella then saw what it was. It was unmistakeably a woman dressed in red with copper-coloured hair. She was holding what looked like a musical instrument.

Kristy spoke before anybody could say anything. "This will astound you. That instrument she is holding... I would put money on it being a kinnor."

"What's a kinnor?" Max looked expectant.

"It's a traditional Jewish harp used since the days of Moses. So, what is one doing on an ancient mural that must be older than the monastery itself?"

There was a stunned silence. They looked around at each other and were all thinking the same thing.

Isabella felt emotional and wiped a tear from her eye. "Oh my God! Could that be the Magdalene? Her cloak, her hair, match descriptions perfectly, and if it's not her then who the bloody hell is it? I've heard stories she carried a harp of sorts. Well done, Kristy. Without you, we would have missed that. It is unbelievable. Let's all take photographs from every possible angle. The more I look at it, the clearer it gets. Oh God, I'm tingling all over!"

Max gave her a hug. "Let's call it a day for now, return tomorrow, and also inform Llama Gyalwang of what we think we may have found. Remember, we are trained researchers, and we accept nothing without evidence. But this is so tempting."

Kristy had a blush of pleasure about her. Her find was without a doubt, of major importance. They all congratulated her on her diligent approach and said she should receive full credit for it. A part of the jigsaw had dropped into place.

That evening, they all sat at the same table in the dining room. The only topic of conversation was the mural depicting the woman with her harp. They did not doubt it was the Magdalene, but they had no way of proving it. Lama Gyalwang was delighted they had found something of importance but was unable offer any explanation. There could be a clue somewhere in the records they were examining but he could not verify it. The more they talked about it, the more excited they became.

Max had a workable solution. "From my cursory glances at various manuscripts, the name Issa does appear in places but not often or for any significant reason. The language they're written in is in a mixture of Pali, Sanskrit, and Tibetan. Using my magnifier, I've made a note of what is written. You will observe that there's a familiar ring to them. I've saved this until now just to see what your reactions would be. Listen to this. *Thus spoke Issa* – part of it is missing and illegible – *with his woman, who stood beside him… Respect all women and your mothers for they are our creators, the mothers of the universe and who did carry us into this world.*

Now, here's another I found… *He, Issa, said we must respect and honour our temple. He meant not that built by men but that of our living heart within us for it is the holiest of places made so by our Parent. We must honour it so, believe it, for it is a gift from God and it lies not.* It all sounds very familiar, doesn't it? But it gets us no nearer to the Magdalene."

Their excitement was not lost on Alexa who, as usual, sat nearby and had even given them a slight smile as she walked in. Every word spoken was being recorded. She too was excited but not for the same reasons. Their find was not something that could be carried away, but its discovery was something that had to be prevented from reaching the outside world. That, for her, meant only one thing – elimination. The following day she was meeting up with Croxley and Marco 'Bull' Morello at the airport, and a plan of action would be decided. She would also be doing a search of their rooms and evidence of what they had found.

Chapter 13

Croxley led a shaky-looking Morello off the aircraft and was beginning to wonder if he had made the right choice. He had never seen Bull behave in this manner, though once on firm ground, he regained his usual presence and began acting as his normal self. That was reassuring.

Waiting for them in the arrivals area was Alexa Heléne. She had left her disguise. Her welcome was without a smile, like she was attending a bankruptcy hearing.

Relating what she had seen and heard, she drove them back to the hotel. "They have found something of importance. It seems to be an ancient mural of a woman holding a Jewish harp. They are almost convinced it's the Magdalene whore and that she was also the bride of our Christ. God cannot forgive such blasphemy. We must take action. They also found references to a man called Issa. They seem to believe he was our beloved Christ, and there were some Biblical-style quotes attributed to this man. It is preposterous. What would you like me to do?"

"When they leave in the morning, that will give you the

chance to get into their room and photograph what you can. Don't take anything from them, for they must not know they are being watched. We will take action when the time comes."

"I will do as you ask, but I am getting restless and would like some action, as I spend most of my time doing nothing."

"That will change. Bull is here because I have a plan which may require his mechanical and digital expertise. Whether I will go ahead with it or not, I am undecided. It depends on what is going on."

"What would that be?"

"From what I hear, the road to this Hemis place is precariously narrow and across a mountain route with dangerous drop-offs over the edge. Bull here knows a thing or two about how to fix a car to have an untraceable accident. Explain it to her, will you, Bull, please?"

With the musicality of his Bronx and slight Italian accent, he began to explain. "I was taught some years back how to fix a Boston brake job. It rarely fails. The Brits invented it, but knowledge is hard to keep quiet. I've done a few in my time. A microchip transceiver is fitted into the steering and braking system. Once activated from a remote distance, it causes a loss of control of steering and braking, often with fatal results. That's all you need to hear. I know how to fit it up and I have all the right equipment and materials."

Alexa looked peeved. "So, am I being denied doing God's work? I am his warrior. Allow me opportunity to fulfil my role in this crusade."

Croxley replied, "We work as a team, and you are not being denied. If it weren't for your work here, we would be none the wiser. I'm certain the opportunities are going to arise for you to use your very special skills. Do not doubt it. When we get to the hotel, show me who these people are and let's

THE MAGDALENE MISSION

look around. We can work it out from there."

"I will do as you ask, but I really do need to practice my skills."

"You will, you will, rest assured."

The head lama was waiting for them when they arrived the next morning. He was holding in his hands a rolled parchment of some age. "We have found this, and I am certain this will be most helpful for you. It is our copy of the Gospel of Saint Issa. Please examine it and we will leave it out for you every day. I believe it is the same one which was used by the man behind your English version, the Russian, Nicholas Notovitch." He handed it over to Isabella.

The team looked at each other in astonishment.

Isabella gave the document the gentlest of kisses. "You are so very kind. You have saved us weeks of work. We cannot thank you enough."

They all gave a big chorus of 'thank you.'

He smiled, lit a cluster of incense, bowed to the manuscript and the company, and let them be.

Max looked shaken. "At last, something positive. This is a mixture of Sanskrit and Pali. They are similar in their sound and sentence constructions. I can't wait to get started and find the pages Notovitch missed, omitted, or couldn't finish."

Kristy spoke. "The lama regards this work with considerable reverence, and we must do the same. Can we work with your book, Bella, and compare it with what is written here and see just how correct his translation was?"

"It goes without saying that we will handle it with

reverence." To their surprise, Max looked at the rolled parchment, placed his palms together, and giving the classic Añjali Mudrā, bowed his head.

Jake began photographing each page up close. "Let me take pictures of the entire parchment and then we will have our own indisputable evidence once we leave this place, and it will be something we can work with later."

She opened the locked door with ease and slid into Jake's room like a ghost on a mission. She wore surgical gloves and carried another digital camera, should she need it. The professor and her colleagues had only just left for dinner, so she had plenty of time to complete her task.

Luck was on her side. Jake's camera was left on the bed. Turning it on, she swiftly found the photographs that had excited them all. She was mindful of Croxley's instructions not to remove anything. Turning off the camera, she connected a USB cable to it and connected the other end to the printer provided by the hotel. There was plenty of photo-printing paper about. Switching on the camera, she went to *Print Settings* and pressed *Print All*. The printer was activated and spat out excellent copies of their work.

She had no idea what it all meant, but she knew it was related to the Magdalene in some way. An hour later, her work was done, and she had excellent printouts of their work. All she had to do before re-joining Croxley and Bull was to switch off the printer.

She didn't totally obey his instructions, and couldn't resist placing the camera, not back on the bed, but on the window

THE MAGDALENE MISSION

ledge. Little things like that, she knew, always had a way of unnerving people or scaring them.

Ten minutes later, she joined both men at her table.

"How did it go? Did you find anything?"

"Masses." She spoke in a hushed whisper, as the professor and others were sitting close by. "I've printed out everything that was on his camera. I'll show you later. What the language is I have no idea, but we can find someone who will know."

"Better still, they can translate it between them. Let them do it, and they are bound to write it down. Once they've done that, we will show them what they are dealing with and then we will have to destroy the evidence – and them with it, if need be. Bull, with his expertise, has the best chance of doing that all in one hit. They appear to be excited from what I can see from here. Whatever they found, it has them pepped up. Start listening in and record every word."

"Jake, did you get the whole manuscript?" Bella asked.

"Everything, and perhaps we will find out why Notovitch didn't complete the entire thing."

"There has to be some reference to the Magdalene somewhere. That piece I read to you mentions Issa's woman. If Issa was Christ, then surely that must be the Magdalene. That mural Kristy discovered was, for me, a clincher, but we need evidence."

"I agree," Max interjected. "With any luck, we might be able to piece together the missing pages of her gospel or find out if they possibly exist somewhere."

"The big puzzle for me, Max, is why the Templars

returned from Jerusalem, and their devotion to John the Baptist and the Magdalene, both patron saints of theirs. There has to be a connection."

"I'll start on the translation tomorrow and see how mine compares with the one in your book. My bet is they will not differ much. I'm more anxious to find what was on the pages he omitted or failed to finish."

Croxley looked at his accomplices. He had heard every word spoken. "We must allow them to do what they came here to do, and then we swoop in, steal it from them, and put paid to them and their activities with no mercy shown. Between us, we have skills they would find hard to believe."

"I need to know what car they use." Bull spoke quietly. "My equipment needs setting-up time, and I don't want anybody interrupting me while I go about it. Let's just watch and listen and we will know when to strike."

"Hold fast, Bull. I need them to succeed and do the work for us. I've decided that it's the most profitable course we can take."

Bull was silent, but his expression said it all.

Chapter 14

The following morning at breakfast, a concerned-looking Jake confronted Isabella.

"There was something most odd when I got back to my room last night. I would have sworn I had placed my camera on the bed pillow. It wasn't there. It had been moved to the other side of the room, and certainly I wouldn't leave it on the window ledge, where I found it."

"Room-service cleaners, most likely, Jake."

"Certainly not, Bella, they don't do night work. And another thing, the printer felt warm, although it was switched off, plus I would have sworn I had much more printing paper than I have right now. I've got a nasty feeling about this."

"You are worrying *me* now. Are you trying to suggest our 'frightener' is here doing this?"

"Exactly. No harm was done, nor was anything stolen when it could have easily been. We'd better talk with Max and Kristy. I could do without this."

Twenty minutes later, they all knew of the situation and agreed to stick close to each other at all times, apart from the bed- and bathrooms.

They set to work on translating and reading through Notovitch's book.

Isabella spoke. "Listen, all of you. Before you get too excited, there's one thing you should know about this book. He was confronted years later about inconsistencies in it."

They all stopped what they were doing.

Max said what they all were thinking, "Are you saying we are wasting our time researching his book?"

"Not exactly, Max. Under pressure, Notovitch allegedly confessed to inventing the whole story. However, there's no evidence that he did so, and many scholars upheld his story. The head lama of the time denied that such a manuscript existed when approached by Western academics. He even denied the existence of Notovitch. So that begs the question, what exactly are we looking at here? There's no doubting its antiquity and That's a point I raised with our current head lama. He told me he had known all along where it was hidden, away from Westerners, many of whom he had little trust in. Notovitch must have seen this, as we are. I'm telling you all this now, as you'd have found out about it later. Our lama trusts and apparently likes us. Remember, while this manuscript exists beyond any shadow of a doubt, our concern is not its authenticity but if there's any way of linking it to the Magdalene and her missing words. So I'm asking you all now, bearing in mind what I've just told you… are you all prepared or not to continue this mission?"

Max stood up and looked at them all. "Nothing I like more than a deepening mystery. Isabella, on hearing that, it makes me more eager than ever. What about you two?" He turned to Kristy and Jake.

In unison they responded, "All the way. No doubting it."

Bella moved across the room and gave them all a hug.

THE MAGDALENE MISSION

"Thank you, thank you all. I was dreading that you might not want to carry on."

An hour passed and not a word was spoken. The only sound was the almost-imperceptible scribbling of notes and the odd mutter.

Max then spoke. "The number of times Israel and Judah are mentioned is substantial. All this buried in the archives of an ancient Tibetan monastery beggars belief. It didn't get there by chance. So far, apart from modern-day idioms and sentence construction, my interpretation is practically identical to what's in Notovitch's book. I don't think it's a fake unless we find evidence to substantiate that. How are the others making out?"

"Pretty much the same," answered Isabella. "What would help would be to find a reference or two to the Magdalene, but so far not even one."

Max held up the piece he was working on. "We have hoards to plough through and some of the writing is illegible. There was that reference to Issa's woman and those passages about honouring all women. We also have many photographs of the woman depicted on the mural. These are substantial clues and, if Issa is Jesus, she could be the Magdalene. If not, then who is it? Also, if Notovitch made up the story, how come we are translating an ancient Pali and Sanskrit text almost identically? He must have seen this, just as we did. That begs the question, then… who wrote the original text? It's mind-blowing and raises more questions than answers."

"I have a feeling our travels are far from over." Bella looked thoughtful.

"Why so?" Kristy asked.

"We may soon possibly think we have found the missing pages, but there's no evidence of that so far. Hopefully, we will find something in Notovitch's work and the pages he never translated. She is, it seems, never mentioned by name. The only proof would be to locate their whereabouts and compare them with what we may find – that is, if they still exist. If so, they would then need to be matched with the Berlin Codex."

"So where do you have in mind?"

"So far, we have been working pretty much in the dark and have had little to go on apart from ancient stories and legends, none of which have a shred of viable evidence. Right now, I think we have made a big stride forward thanks to our head lama. There may be truths in some of those ancient stories yet. Once finished here, and hopefully with revelatory material, I foresee a trip back to Jerusalem. If my ideas are correct, we may possibly also be making a trip to Italy, France, Portugal, or even the UK."

"What are you thinking?" Jake asked.

"Those pages were removed deliberately and for a particular reason. Think about it. Who would want to do a thing like that and why? The only people who possibly could have, were Emperor Constantine and the Council of Nicaea in 325 AD, the newly formed Roman Catholic Church, and the Knights Templar. Between the first two, the Gospel of Mary was expunged from canonical texts, as were those of Philip and Thomas. The fact that there were no crucifixions or divine miracles mentioned probably had much to do with it. Yet the Templars almost worshipped the Magdalene, and she was their patron saint even though the church, at the time, had branded her a prostitute, a common whore. Only later in this century, in 1919 and then in 1969, did they admit that there was no Biblical evidence to support the allegation."

"Okay," Kristy looked puzzled, "so why would the

THE MAGDALENE MISSION

Templars remove such pages?"

"Good question. As they revered her so, it seems they had access to what she or someone else had written. The only place they could have done that was in Jerusalem or Rome, where the gospels were allegedly found. There were writings they did not want the church to discover. The Templars were prepared to die for her and keep all hostile eyes away from her seemingly controversial statements or, in the church's eyes, the ridiculous concept of blasphemy, punishable by torture followed by death." She paused and opened her hands. "How am I doing?"

Max looked across at Jake and Kristy and they both nodded. "Bella, I feel as these two do – excited, inspired, and ready to press on harder."

All their fears were forgotten, and any sense of danger left them.

One floor above them, Croxley was filing his fingernails into perfect symmetry.

Nearby sat Bull, cleaning his Glock 17 handgun, complete with a fitted suppressor, with loving care. "When do we strike?" he asked, peering down the short gun barrel. "I'm getting twitchy."

"We don't do anything until they discover something, and that could take some weeks yet. Both of you two are far too eager right now. Your time will come, rest assured. Alexa reports that they seem excited, so I guess they may be onto something. When they next leave, she will go through all their rooms and attempt to find what is causing their excitement."

"Well, I hope it's soon, or this boy could do something rash."

"Please don't. I'm paying you well and I don't want you upsetting God's task. Remember, we are his soldiers, and he speaks through me. You may be his mercenary, Bull, but you are under my command. You only do things when I tell you to and not before. Have you got that loud and clear?"

A flicker of anger crossed Bull's face. He wasn't used to being spoken to in such a manner. "Yeah, I got it, but a little accident happening to one of them would do a little damage and help relieve the boredom."

Croxley knew he had to keep his soldiers happy. "I'll think about it and will give you a reply soon. Meanwhile, sit tight."

Bull managed a slight smile. So… all was not lost.

Chapter 15

A number of days passed, and there were no great revelations until they reached the section that, for some reason, did not appear to be translated.

Max spoke first. "Notovitch was a scholar, and either he ran out of time or … But no scholar would leave off in such a fashion. They would go on until it was completed. My bet is that he did work on it, and it was completed."

"Why didn't he include it, then?" Isabella asked.

"My guess is it was too controversial. If made common knowledge, and with more than a hint of truth in it, the entire edifice of the Catholic hierarchy and many other Christian faiths could have come tumbling down, together with great sections of the established canonical structure. Films like *The Da Vinci Code* would be spot-on with their assumptions."

All three leant in closer.

"Well, what have you found?" Kristy asked.

"I've only just started… and listen to this. I will have to go back over it several times to make sure I've got it right. This section seems to have been written by somebody else and there's no clue as to who that might have been. Make of it what you will." He proceeded to read.

Thus did Issa the honoured one turn and kiss his companion upon her mouth. Magda then turned and spoke to the gathered disciples, and she did speak of Issa. "Think of him in your hearts and in your minds. Full of great compassion he must always be prayed to. To calls from every quarter he responds.

"The next part is so faded it's illegible. However, here's the next section. Just wait until you hear this." Max was brimming with excitement. "We have the living words of Issa – or, as we suspect, Christ – as spoken by him directly."

Thus did Issa turn to Magda, his companion. "Your question on the reality of life is one of great depth and beyond the understanding of many, but you have grasped it." He turned to his audience. "Know you this. Through my Parent, God knows that all our senses and thoughts are empty. Dear ones, know that there is neither suffering nor can there be disease, old age, or death. Thus, Magda has seen that form is no more than emptiness and emptiness is as form. They are as one and not so at all times."

That's as far as I've got and there's more to come yet."

There was a stunned silence. Bella wiped a tear from her eye. "We have proof. Oh my God, I'm shaken beyond belief. 'Magda' has to be her. She must be. She must be!"

"No doubting it. No hesitancy at all in agreeing with that." Jake looked confident. "What do you make of it all, Max?"

"I have a theory, which is the only one I can come up with. What I am working on is for certain the missing content, which should fit in with her gospel in the Berlin Museum. The mystery is, who removed it? I suspect there was a religious motive, but why, and what was done with it? But then why was the remainder left intact? The Gospel of Mary is, as we know, a non-canonical text discovered in 1896 in a fifth-century papyrus codex and is written in Sahidic Coptic. That's

THE MAGDALENE MISSION

written as a modified form of the Greek alphabet with several additional letters borrowed from the Demotic Egyptian script. How her text got written down this way is a mystery and I can only guess it must have come directly from her original scribe or even herself. She was, by all accounts, literate and fluent in several languages and dialects.

"A German diplomat, Carl Reinhardt, purchased this Berlin Codex in Cairo. I think we need to retrace it back to Jerusalem and see if we have missed something. I really want to see the missing text in its original form. If it still exists. I also think the Templars and Pope Gregory knew more than we have been led to believe."

Max leant forward to make his point. "What we have here is written in Sanskrit by monks of old, in response to what they heard. To verify it, we need to see the Sahidic-Coptic version. If found and if it matches up, we have the greatest find since the Dead Sea Scrolls. So, let's press on."

The only sound was the click of her camera. She had been through all their rooms and taken shots of every note, page of scripts, research material, and their planned agenda. Unable to resist the temptation, she made a swift, precise, neat slash through the top page of Max's research notes on Buddhist and Hindu scriptures with her scalpel. She had not been able to understand a word of them, but her cut epitomised how she felt about its effrontery to God Almighty. Ten minutes later, she presented her findings to Croxley.

He scanned every shot with great care, especially the translation of the missing piece, knowing that there would be more to come. "I don't like this at all. It's a mass of heresy and blasphemy and cannot be allowed to be seen by anybody. We have two options – destroy every note and photograph ... But with the internet and digital technology that, at times, is almost an impossibility. What they are doing is presenting the false gods of a heathen, pagan, and backward people as the truth. They must be stopped before any more damage is done."

Bull became alert. "Brake job, boss?"

"I am not certain. They are discovering too much, I feel. Your time could be arriving. We can easily dispose of their notes, but Ignatius wants to see everything first. We don't want to disappoint him, now, do we?"

Alexa was deeply disappointed. She felt redundant.

"Hey, would you look at that." Max held up the top sheet of his research notes to reveal a perfect diagonal slash from end to end. "How the hell did that happen? I didn't leave it like that. It looks as if it has been done deliberately."

"Oh God!" Bella blurted out. "It must have been our unknown stalker at work here. I am now convinced of it. All these scary episodes are no coincidence. Whoever it is must be here somewhere in this hotel."

"You are right, but who can it be?"

"Most seem to be tourists from all over. It could be anyone. Someone, somewhere, doesn't seem to want us to do what we are doing."

"Have you seen anyone who seems to be acting suspiciously?"

THE MAGDALENE MISSION

"What about that woman with the dark shades and blonde hair who always seems to sit near us? She arrived the same day as us. She now has two male companions. They all sound American."

"That's a good point. They could possibly hear everything we say and discuss."

"True. They seem to have a God-squad look about them, don't you think?"

"I think you are right, but surely they couldn't be doing such things?"

"Well, don't take that for granted. Religious nutters and cult organisations litter the last century. You only have to look at outfits like the Branch Davidians, the Heaven's Gate screwballs, and the Peoples Temple bunch to know all things gross and evil are entirely possible in the name of religion and God."

"So, what do we do?"

"Let's call in Kristy and Jake and see what they have to say."

One hour later, all their fears and suspicions had been outlined and it was decided that their anxieties were centred on the American trio.

Later that evening, they were seated at their usual table and the three Americans sat, as expected, close by. Her 'phone' was on the table, picking up and recording every word.

Bella and the others all, at various times, shot glances around the dining room, making certain they got a good look at the three.

The woman removed her shades and began rubbing her eyes, as they appeared swollen.

Jake looked startled.

Careful not to talk, he scribbled a note and passed it to Max. It said, 'I think I know who that is. *It's the woman who kept staring and smiling at me a while back. It's her face, but the hair is different. She must be wearing a syrup! It has to be her!*'

Max read it and let out a low whistle, then passed it to Bella.

Her jaw dropped and she covered her mouth with her hand, Kristy following suit.

Without a word, Max stood and gestured to them all to follow. Once outside, he spoke. "We are leaving here in the morning. This is too dangerous. I'll book a flight back to Jerusalem, and a hotel for when we get there. We are not driving back to Hemis. I will contact the lama and explain this to him. Our safety is at risk here. I've also translated most of the bits missing from Notovitch's book. They are amazing. I can see why he didn't include them. I will tell you all later. Bella, am I jumping the gun here? If so, I apologise."

"No need, Max. I think we are all in total agreement and need to get out of here fast before God knows what nasty things may happen to us. Full steam ahead."

Chapter 16

Croxley bellowed and smashed his fist hard on the tabletop. "They're gone! They're gone! They left with their entire luggage and in a hired people carrier. We have lost them, damn it! Where the hell are they heading?"

Bull said nothing, but disappointment etched his face. He had no idea.

Alexa looked thoughtful. She half suspected her handiwork had caused the exodus. On that, she had a shrewd idea. From what she had managed to pick up about the Templars, it had to be Jerusalem. She outlined her reasoning to Croxley.

"I think you might be right." He looked thoughtful as well. "There are a few things to work out. Where will they be staying? We can't all be seen together. They must have noticed us all. Ending up in the same hotel together would give the game away. My bet is they will go back to where they stayed last time. We need to split up. They must have seen you every day."

"Yes, but I've been disguised. I have other disguises and

ruses that have never been detected in the past. Let me go, and remember... I'm the only one here with long-distance tracking and listening devices."

"Okay, but make sure you do not resemble the person they saw every day. We will stay elsewhere close by."

"I heard also they mentioned the town of Magda, plus France, and Portugal. I think they must have found out something, for they all seemed excited."

"We will soon find out, and whatever it is must never see the light of day and be destroyed either by us or Bishop Ignatius. Are we all agreed?"

There was no dissent.

"That's good. I'll report back to Ignatius and when that's done, we will sort out hotels and flights."

An unhappy expression crossed Bull's face.

Three Days Later
Villa Brown Hotel
Jerusalem

The manager was more than delighted that his previous guests had returned to his hotel in spite of the mishaps that occurred not so long ago. It said good things to him, and he went out of his way to ensure their comfort and safety. He gave them the best rooms available, a permanently reserved restaurant table, and two bottles of his finest wine.

Seated at their table, Bella said what they all felt. "I'm glad we have found our way back here. I was beginning to get jumpy in India. Those three Americans were definitely suspicious."

"Recognising that woman was a clincher," Jake piped up.

"I wouldn't be surprised," Kristy added, "if she had a listening device of some sort."

Max put his notebook on the table. "You have been seeing too many 007 movies, Kristy. All of you, before I discuss my translation with you, I want to hear what your theories are regarding the Templar connection."

It was at that moment the manager appeared and gave them a friendly wave as he led a grey-haired disabled lady walking with a stick to a nearby table.

They all smiled and returned his cheerful wave.

Bella leant forward. "Well, this is my theory, and this is why I wanted to get here. It was something we missed. Excavations around Temple Mount have been going on for years. Last week or so, they found a perfectly preserved Templar sword and shield, which we ought to take a look at. The Templars adored and almost worshipped the Magdalene. She was, for them, the feminine sign of God Almighty. Her story is no different from a host of pagan rituals, which are often represented by a circle – the womb, if you like. It became the universally accepted symbol of womanhood. The church felt threatened, and the Templars were a powerful force and extremely wealthy. The Magdalene was declared a whore by a male-dominated religion. The Gospels of Thomas, Philip, and Mary were cast out – they made no mention of a virgin birth, wise men, miracles, and the crucifixion and so on. The Magdalene understood Jesus in a way the disciples could not. The Templars were in awe of her. Their church in London is round, circular-built as a salutation to her femininity, the female aspect of God the Parent, as is the French Church – also in London – which is also circular. So alarmed was the church that it declared circular constructions in churches heretical. They went a step further and they were banned."

The disabled lady began an extended bout of coughing.

"Okay." Jake looked confused. "Well, good stuff, but what's that got to do with what we are looking for?"

Max broke his silence. "I think it has everything to do with it, Jake. You will see in a minute. My theory is that the Templars removed the sections that were most controversial and, to the church, a threat. They could even have come from the original itself. From what I've translated, it is heady stuff indeed, and Issa – or Jesus – is addressing a woman who, as you have already heard, is named as Magda. Where those missing pages may be and where they went, who knows, or if they even still exist. Do you want to hear my translation?"

They all nodded an enthusiastic assent.

"Here goes. Sit back and listen." He opened up his notebook. "This is how I read it. Whoever wrote it, there's no disputing what was being said. Issa is addressing her. As he makes clear, she was indeed exceptional and his true disciple. This was difficult, as there was no punctuation or grammatical structure. Words all joined up with each other and there were no capital letters. It has taken me a long time, but this is what I gathered.

Thus did Issa speak to her, his companion, Magda. He spoke that all could hear him. He said, "Know this and you will tell the people these simple truths." She sat to listen.

"Know, Magda, and those who have ears to hear that from East to West flowed from the mind of God's greatest sage these simple truths and to the source were kept pure as an unsullied stream. Within all light there's darkness. Light goes with darkness, as do the steps in the sequence of our walking. Do not set up your own

standards for the path to God is clear, no matter how far you may walk. As you walk on, distinctions between near and far are lost.

"I offer great truth. Do not waste time, oh Magda. Behold, there's no void. There's no form, sensation, or thought. Nor is there perception, nor sound, colour, or what the mind takes hold. No consciousness, taste, touch, or ignorance and knowledge.

"Know this, Magda, there's no old age, disease, suffering, or death. These, in their true nature, are unreal. These things will not be felt. God, our Parent, both male and female, is indeed wonderful. Magda, you walk the path, and you will forever walk it. Going on, always going on, going on beyond, and always beyond."

Max stopped. All around him was an astonished silence. "Look, guys, there are many more pages, all in a similar style. I confess I don't truly understand them, but here is a profundity of spiritual insight, a sort of mystical wisdom not found in the Gospels. I guess it was too much for Constantine and his male retinue to swallow, and later the church. I found it moving in a way I would never have believed." He lowered his head.

The silence was broken from close by as the disabled woman began limping from her table with a handkerchief over her nose and mouth, coughing and spluttering furiously.

For a moment, nothing was said as they turned to look at her, but she limped off as fast as she could.

Bella was the first to speak. "That's groundbreaking material, Max, and throws up all sorts of possibilities. We know the Templar knights had their HQ at the Temple, and if Mary's gospel were there, they would undoubtedly have seen it. Many of them were learned scholars and saw themselves as God's elite protective force. We must go and see that shield and sword and have a chat with the excavation director – Professor Jacob Levi, if I remember correctly. He may be able to give us more information. Max, I think your evaluation of what might have happened is a sound one, but without primary evidence of some sort, all our speculation doesn't add up to a hill of beans. Add to this the threats our stalker has given us, and we are on the horns of a dilemma, don't you think?"

"The sooner we get started, the better. We've done enough talking. We now need some action," Max agreed.

The following morning was warm and humid, and the city was thronging with thousands of people from across the world. For a stalker – or worse, a murderer – it was the ideal place in which to hide and not be noticed. Bull was happy about that as he elbowed his way through a group of pilgrims. Acting on what Alexa had told them, he was heading for the excavation site close to the holy temple. He knew they had arranged to meet Professor Jacob Levi, the site director. He had no idea at what time but, whatever, he would wait. He was good at waiting. As long as he felt the snug warmth of his suppressed Glock pistol in his shoulder holster, he felt happy with the world.

He was under strict instructions from Croxley that he must only shoot to scare but not harm in any way. If that didn't drive them off, then the stakes would be raised for a deadlier game.

Pushing his way past endless crowds, he reached the excavation site. As expected, it was heavily sealed off with yellow and black tape. Within the area, he could see teams of workers, some kneeling and scraping, others measuring and examining various finds, all placed on an array of trestle tables. These were positioned inside two enormous marquee-style tents, complete with twenty-four-hour security guards.

He scoured the area, shielding his eyes from the sun's glare. There was no sign of them. Finding a nearby flat rock behind a small stone pillar, he sat down. It gave him a full-scale view of the activities whilst keeping him out of sight. He gave a relaxed sigh. Being in the open air gave him an escape from the claustrophobic confines of cabins and walls. He patted his shoulder holster and pulled out a small hip flask. A few gulps of scotch and he felt good. All he needed now was his quarry.

He didn't have long to wait.

The four of them, he could see, were admitted into the sealed area and greeted by a short, rotund, bespectacled man wearing a large khaki jungle hat who had men running around him. He was obviously the director, and he led the four of them into one of the large tents.

It was time for action.

"This way." Jacob Levi ushered his guests inside. "We have retained the sword and shield for further examination. Considering its age, it is in remarkable condition. After close examination, we could even make out the etched signature of sorts of whomever must have owned this."

"Oh." Isabella's eyes widened and her jaw dropped. "I can't wait to see it!"

Max and the other two all looked astonished. "You mean it can be read?"

"Yes," replied the director. "Due to the dryness and the quality of the sand and dirt around it, it withstood the test of time. Look, we're here."

In front of them stood a large wooden crate, which had been wrapped in a blanket of polystyrene. He carefully removed the protective layer and gently pulled open the lid to reveal a worn and dirty-looking shield and a large sword in a similar condition. He explained the circumstances of the find, where it was found, and the implications of such a discovery. The shield looked battle scarred, with many dents, but was remarkably rust-free. On the front was the unmistakeable faded outline of the Templars' insignia, a stylised red cross.

The sword was far from smooth and had obviously, by the chips in the blade, seen action of some sort.

"Look here," said the director, pointing to a faintly observable etching along the blade's edge. "We cleaned it up as carefully and gently as we could. I believe it could be a signature."

"Let's see." Max produced his loupe eyepiece and bent closer to examine it. "I think you are right." He stood up. "It looks like medieval script. Let me write it down." Several minutes later he spoke again. "It seems to spell out a name,

THE MAGDALENE MISSION

that of Percy de Havilland."

They all crowded around to look at it.

The first bullet hit the top of the nearby shield, followed by a second and then a third. For a moment they froze. There had been no sound of a gunshot, just lead ripping through steel.

Max roared, "Down, everyone, we're being shot at!"

They pressed down hard and urgently into the sand as a fourth bullet went through the trestle table holding the shield.

"Jesus Christ!" Isabella shouted, looking as white as snow. She dropped to the ground. "Who the hell can be shooting at us?"

No one spoke.

They lay where they were for several minutes until all had gone quiet. The director was shaking, and the entire group looked shocked.

Jake cautiously lifted his head to get a clearer view. "There's nobody out there. It's empty."

With great care and slowness, they all began standing.

Max was still holding the sword. He placed it down and looked carefully around.

Jacob Levi broke the shocked silence. "Clearly someone does not like what we are doing here."

"It looks that way, Professor. Will you inform the police?"

"Of course, I will. I've no idea who they are or why they should shoot at us."

Isabella looked at her colleagues with a raised eyebrow. They looked questioningly at each other. She held a finger to her lips and shook her head. They knew what she was thinking. She turned to the director and explained that they had better leave, then thanked him profusely and implored him to immediately report the incident to the police.

He gave them permission to take photographs of both shield and sword. They then made their way back to the hotel and not a word was spoken between them.

He chuckled quietly to himself. It had been a job well done and if that didn't go a long way towards getting them to leave, then sterner measures would be needed. He repositioned himself out of sight to watch reactions. What he saw amused him. A group of anxious and nervous-looking people slowly pulled themselves upwards and began frantically scanning in all directions. He could have taken any one of them out. He rarely missed, but now he was obeying orders.

Later, he related the episode to both Croxley and Alexa, whose expression was one of suppressed jealousy.

"That's encouraging." Croxley ran his hand through his thinning hair. "It now remains to be seen what they will do next. Maybe they will abandon the exercise and we can draw a curtain across it." He turned to Alexa. "You know what you have to do. Listen in again and find out what they are planning and then report back to me."

That evening, the research team sat at their usual table. There was an uneasy atmosphere between them. The events of the day had been traumatic.

Bella broke the silence. "I guess we're all thinking the same thing. What I'm going to say next, please think long and hard about it. It's important. It's clear that ever since we started on this mission there's somebody – or several somebodies – who, for some unknown reason, does not want us to proceed. We have had dangerous scare attacks of all sorts ever since we started, and to top those off, today we have been shot at. Our lives are in danger. Is it time we gave up? Any of you are perfectly free to leave without any recriminations. I will respect whatever decision you make. Personally, I've been torn as to what would be the wisest course of action. Yet, as we know from history, wise decisions are often the worst to make. To make progress, risks have to be taken. So, I hope you can understand where I'm at." She leant back in her seat and gazed at the three of them. The sound of loud coughing caused her to turn and look at whoever it was. All she could see was the elderly lady with her walking stick who they had seen the previous evening. She had a menu in one hand and a phone to her ear.

She stopped coughing and took several deep breaths, then put down the phone, yet her lips continued to move as if in silent prayer. Bella's words and those of the others were coming through loud and clear. *What are they going to decide? I hope they stay!*

Kristy spoke first. "I speak for both me and Jake. We discussed this possibility earlier and we wish to continue. We want to find Rabbi Cohen once more. There are a few things I want to ask him, such as what he knows about the Knights Templar and what happened. It seems all of history has been passed down through his family, from before the Crusades and after. I think we may find something of interest and of help. What do you think?"

Max interjected, "I'm no hero, and my first thought was, 'Let's get the hell out of here, it's too risky.' Life's more important than chasing rainbows and unsubstantiated stories." He paused and looked at them all. "We've been scared shitless and now shots have been fired at us. There are powerful people at play here and we are at their sharp end. Reasoning tells me this has to be a religious mission of sorts to prevent Magdalene's missing work from emerging. Sure, I have translations of Notovitch's omitted pages, but – but – the academic world is never going to accept that unless they see the primary evidence. I can't shove this aside. We need to follow up on every scrap of information, no matter how irrelevant, bizarre, unscientific – or scientific – it may appear. There's an answer here somewhere and I really want to find it. So, you can guess what my answer is!" He slapped the table.

The disabled lady smiled into her wine glass, wiped her lips, and listened as they made plans. Pushing back her chair, she gave a few more coughs and hobbled out of the dining room. Already, in her head, there were images forming of locations, activities, and exactly how they would be handled. Pressing against her belly in its protective case, she felt the comforting presence of her titanium scalpel, which was about to be summoned for God's duty and that of his beloved son, Jesus Christ. Sinners and unbelievers were destined for death and eternal Hell.

Croxley listened intently to what she was telling him. His eyes glinted and a thoughtful look crossed his face. "I think they're warming to their task. So far, they haven't given up and from what you say, they don't look as though they will. They seem determined to press on regardless of the perils that they

THE MAGDALENE MISSION

suspect may await them. We'll not disappoint them on that score. Let them go to Magdala and bring back whatever they find. That will save us a trip. Once they have gone, we'll look around their rooms again. You can cut something, and you, Bull, can place a couple of bullets in their rooms. That should give them something to think about."

Chapter 17

Magdala
The Following Morning

As ever, the sun shone brightly around the rolling hills and off the magnificent blue of the Sea of Galilee. Both Bella and Max were surprised to see that what had once been an ancient fishing village was now transformed into a busy, bustling municipality. Kristy and Jake led them to the on-going excavation site around the aged Migdal Synagogue. Here they would see once more the alleged Magdalene's house before making enquiries concerning Rabbi Cohen.

"He said he was local and had lived here his total life and all that has happened in this place since the time of Christ has eternally been handed down from generation to generation, and he is currently the latest in the line of custodians of that knowledge. He must be known here." Jake scanned the area to see if there was any sign of him.

"Let's ask someone." Kristy looked hopeful.

"No need." Jake spoke. "I can see him now." He pointed to some nearby slabs of granite and there, reading, sat Rabbi

THE MAGDALENE MISSION

Cohen.

He looked up as they approached, gave a smile of recognition, and stood up.

Jake made the introductions and handshakes went all around before Jake explained the reason they had been looking for him.

"So, you want to know if, from my family and ancestors, I know anything about the Templars? Sure, well, we do have stories about them, and most are violent and unpleasant, but that didn't stop or prevent us from observing their customs and ways. How reliable they are, who can tell? Is there a particular aspect you're interested in?"

Isabella then explained in meticulous detail about their search and their quest for the missing segments of the Magdalene's gospel and why they were doing it and the events that had occurred since they began their search.

The rabbi looked thoughtful. "Let's all sit down, and I will tell you what I know. You Christians are bewildering, but I've heard stories relating to this. Your Templars were followers of her more than your Christ. That's well known. They were persecuted at the end of the thirteenth century or early fourteenth. Their pope, together with King Philip of France, was afraid of their power and jealous of their vast wealth. Much of that was stolen from us. The Grand Master of the Templars was a man named Jacques de Molay. He was tortured, but later retracted his confession. For that, he was burnt to death on a scaffold on an island in the river Seine. There, his remains gradually rotted and blew away as dust and ashes. It is said he had many supporters who apparently got onto the island and found, unbelievably, that his heart had remained unharmed. Secretly, it was taken to the Temple Mount in Jerusalem. This is the story handed down to us from that time so long ago. You choose what you believe. It was said that it survived the long journey and remained intact. There were still Templars in our city. They supposedly took his heart and placed it in a casket made of pure gold. But that wasn't the only thing that was placed in it. Several rolls of papyrus were included. It was then sealed with bitumen and wax. We are told that it was taken through Egypt and then, we presume, into Europe. Where, we cannot say. It was said it got to Portugal and then to France and even Scotland. Who knows? Does this help you, and is it what you wanted to hear? It is the same story that my ancestral line has told time and time again across centuries."

They looked at each other, astonished.

"Bloody hell!" Max sounded amazed. "Yes, we knew he was burnt at the stake, but we have never heard that part of the story before. Wow."

"What was the papyrus that went with it? What was that all about? Are you all thinking what I'm thinking?"

They agreed. Could it be the missing parts of Mary's gospel?

"There's a little more," Rabbi Cohen continued. "It was said that her gospel was written in stages. Some think part of it was written in India, and others in Jerusalem and Judea. The Templars, amongst the riches they obtained, managed to locate the Gospel of Mary Magdalene and stole it. For them, no doubt a great prize. Mary Magdalene was a figure – their saint – who they were devoted to with all their might, their strength, along with John the Baptist… more than Jesus. They had erudite scholars in their ranks who could have translated the work. They knew the Catholic Church from Rome would never condone this, and her work risked destruction. Such was their veneration that they removed the most controversial

THE MAGDALENE MISSION

parts. The Templars revered her gospel so much before it vanished, until it was discovered in Egypt in the late nineteenth and early twentieth century – minus the missing parts – the story of which, I am sure you know. It would seem her gospel was left in the East where the Catholic Church would not find and destroy it. Perhaps the missing parts were hidden with his heart and sealed up."

"That's the best lead we've had since we got here. First the discoveries at Hemis, and when we were beginning to flounder, you, Rabbi, have given us an amazing and compelling story."

Max let out a long, low whistle. "What you have said, Rabbi, explains many things. That you have had this story handed down across the ages and we in the West have never heard it before, is astonishing."

"It looks like we may be looking for a casket instead of a buried papyrus of sorts." Bella sounded animated. "I wasn't expecting that. Where on earth do we start?"

Kristy added her view. "The Templars could not possibly have remained in France. Although the Magdalene was reported to have spent her remaining years leading a solitary life in a French cave, centuries before the Templars came on the scene. Several other stories contradict that, and the suspected cave has been searched and excavated and nothing has ever been found. To believe the Magdalene narrative, you have to take on board the theory that Jesus did not perish on the cross. That he and she fled to Egypt, then to Italy, France, Portugal, and even somewhere in the UK to escape further ordeals. The Templar adoration came much later, with the Crusades. There are several Templar churches dotted around Europe. Listen closely… near Treviso in Northern Italy is a Templar church, *Tempio di Ormelle*. It depicts the Magdalene, with a red cloak, presenting Jesus with an infant." Kristy paused.

"Please, carry on." Isabella was eager for more.

"Well, what does that suggest? It suggests that the infant was theirs and like all good Jewish men, he would have been married to her. The church has put out their version of the event. It was not the Magdalene but the Virgin Mary in an act of *Dormitio Virginis*. It is the death of the Virgin Mary and Jesus, her son, receives her soul in the form of a baby. I think that interpretation goes too far. Acceptance of the Templar view was not a starter for the Church. Would the casket be in this place? Who knows? That's all I can say about it, but before I finish, there's a work, similar in every detail, by the artist Jacopo Torriti in the Basilica di Santa Maria Maggiore in Rome, and I've seen it. Breathtaking in its implications, is all I can say. Its colours are deeply significant."

Kristy continued. "Magdalene was often shown in red robes and wearing a green dress of sorts. Green symbolised eternal life, the colour of paradise and also hope, and the promise of eternal life in heaven. Green was often used in this respect in early Christian art. Let me show you what a red-robed Magdalene might have looked like."

She reached into her backpack and produced a small book. "Look here." She showed them a picture. "It's full of symbolised meaning."

Max looked impressed. "I agree, but it doesn't get us any closer to finding what we want. Besides, because an artist paints it that way doesn't mean it's true, does it?"

THE MAGDALENE MISSION

Mary Magdalene, Orthodox Icon

The rabbi added more. "Your search is intriguing. We in this country are not enamoured with robbers like the Knights Templar. Their legacy has been written in our blood, but your story of Mary Magdalene is of great interest to us here in Magdala. You must tell us what you find. Will you promise me that?"

Isabella nodded vigorously and reached out to him. "Of course, you will be the first to know. You have given us information we had never known before and that gives us a new dimension and an idea where we might go next."

Their goodbyes were warm and cordial, with promises to meet again in the future.

Chapter 18

There was little difficulty in accessing their vacant rooms. Bull had spare bullets and a silencer fitted to his Glock 17 handgun. He signalled Alexa to stand well back as he fired two shots, one into each of the pillows. There was only a muffled sound like the last gasp of a dying man. He gave a satisfied smile as he dropped two live rounds onto their pillows. Not a word was said.

Alexa, using her titanium-bladed scalpel, carefully, and with all the love she could muster, inscribed with deep cuts four crucifixes, one for each of them, across their luggage carriers. Next, using her red lipstick, she smeared large crucifix imagery across all the mirrors. A buzz of pleasure passed through her at the thought that she was being active once more.

She looked across at Bull. He was smiling and stroking the suppressor on his pistol. "Bull, I think we have done some good work here. If this doesn't cause a reaction, nothing will."

"Well, you will be closer to the reaction than me and Matthew. I'm sure you'll let us know. So, let's get out of here before they return, and report back to our hotel."

When they arrived, Croxley listened to their story with a look of pleasure. "I would love to see their reaction. Something tells me they will be out of here by tomorrow morning. We need to know where. It's over to you."

Isabella and Max stood in shocked, speechless silence for what seemed like an eternity.

"Oh my God!" Isabella shrieked with her hand over her mouth. The crucifixes on the mirrors and the slashed luggage needed no interpretation.

"Jesus H Christ!" roared Max. "They are back in the hotel. Look!" He held up two pillows with bullet holes neatly drilled into them, together with two live rounds lying side by side. "Holy Shit. They want us off the mission, whoever they are. Jake and Kristy. I must—" Before he could finish, they burst into the room. They looked traumatised.

"You too!" Jake spluttered, with a frantic-looking Kristy hanging on to his arm.

"Yes, we are being given a very obvious warning. Our research is upsetting some people. But who?" He picked up the phone and called the manager and security guards. Within minutes, they arrived.

There was no explanation from the frantic manager, who immediately called the police and posted some of the security guards on the team's doors.

"Let's get to the bar and talk this through urgently." Isabella was white with anxiety. "C'mon, let's go."

The manager stepped in front of them. "You will not be charged for anything you drink or eat, and the police will

THE MAGDALENE MISSION

want to speak with you."

They sat at the bar for thirty minutes being questioned by the police, and were not able to give them any leads, apart from their suspicions of an American trio, one of whom had disguised herself and had been seen frequently in close proximity to them. Jake told them all he knew and had seen. There was little to go on.

They were left on their own.

"What do we do now?" asked Kristy.

"We get the hell out of here." Max spat out his words with venom.

"We need to vote again on whether we want to continue with this mission or not," Jake suggested.

Bella spoke next. "It's clear we are in danger of injury or even death if we continue. We have had this vote before but now it seems the stakes have been raised. I, for one, will go along with whatever you decide. Personally, I feel we should get out of here and head for Rome and then on to France, or wherever. We've come so far, I don't want to stop now. We have tantalising new information and I want to follow up on it, come what may."

Nearby sat the usual disabled lady, who gave them a cheery wave with one hand, and with the other she held a phone to her ear.

The team gave her a polite smile and returned the gesture.

"I'm scared." Kristy spoke in a loud whisper. "But I'm not going to give in to a bunch of what I see as religious nutters."

Jake placed a reassuring arm around her. "We are with

you, sweetheart, one hundred percent, are we not?" He looked at the others.

They nodded.

"Tomorrow, we head off to Rome and I suspect we will then be off elsewhere, and we should have a better idea what to do from there. What do you all think?" Bella looked at them questioningly.

There was no disagreement.

"Santa Maggiore it is, then. Perhaps that painting you saw, Kristy, may give us a clue."

A loud crash then startled them. They were hyper jittery. All four bent low only to see that the disabled lady had dropped both a glass and her metal walking cane to the floor. Another guest was helping her pick them up as she made to leave.

"Shit!" Max looked anxious. "We've all become stressed out."

"After what's been happening to us, it's hardly surprising." Bella's colouring remained pale. "Let's get some stiff drinks in before we freeze with fright."

They barely noticed the disabled lady heading out at a faster pace than she looked capable of.

Chapter 19

The following day, the three-and-a-half-plus hour flight to Rome's Fiumicino Airport passed without incident. They remained on full alert. Every ten minutes or so, Bella and Max would scan around the plane and Jake would walk the aisle to see if there was any woman resembling the one he had seen in Jerusalem. They found nothing of interest. It seemed their stalkers had been given the slip.

They travelled from the airport to their hotel, the four-star Hotel Morgana. It was in close proximity to the Basilica.

Kristy shuddered on hearing the hotel name. "That name gives me the willies."

"What's wrong with that?" Jake asked.

"She was part of Arthurian legend, and she often lurks at the fringes of the Arthurian court, plotting its downfall and that of Arthur and his queen. She was responsible for his fatal wounding."

"What's that got to do with our quest?"

"I'm not sure, but she was evil and, given what we have been going through, that name hardly seems an appropriate choice."

"Believe in the heraldic statement, I say. *'Honi soit qui mal y pense.'* But I don't mean you, Kristy. You are a scientist, not a witch or an evil cow. Put it behind you, now."

She shrugged and they all proceeded to check in to their respective rooms. If they had bothered to look around, they would have noticed a woman across the square focussing a powerful pair of binoculars on them all.

The Italian sun was, as usual, hot and sticky, and birds alighted on warm surfaces with caution. Tourists wore sun hats, some carried fans, and all sought the shady tables that were dotted around the numerous colourful squares and fountains.

Seated in a terrace close to the Basilica Santa Maria Maggiore in the Antico Caffe Santamaria was the portly figure of Bishop Ignatius, head of the secret Department for Investigating Suspected Heresies, aka DISH. Being on home territory, he felt very much at ease. He was expecting a meeting with Matthew Croxley and his two assistants. His wait was not long. Three figures, all wearing wide-brimmed hats and dark glasses, headed directly towards him. He recognised Croxley at once, along with Alexa, but not the third. He rose to greet them. "My friends, welcome to Rome." He quickly made the sign of the cross and noticed their discomfort at the same time.

Croxley took the opportunity to introduce an embarrassed-looking Bull, who was plainly uneasy with all things Catholic. After ordering their drinks, he explained to the bishop what progress they had made and what they had learnt from listening in to their conversations.

Ignatius looked thoughtful. "From what you say, it is clear they think they are on to something, and they may well be. If we scare them off or whatever, we may never know what they could have found. I suggest you continue to let them know of your presence, by whatever means you choose, but my patience is limited. We, the church, would like them to think they have something. Then we'll destroy its falsehoods once and for all. The world will know nothing of its obscenity or of them, as you will eliminate them how you see fit. Whatever happens, the church and our faith must not be brought into this, or even be suspected of being involved. Now, having got this far, is that understood?"

Alexa gave a smile of pure pleasure and Bull nodded. They were being given permission to have fun.

Croxley spoke. "We know they are here, and they will be going to the Basilica Santa Maria Maggiore to inspect a painting. We will watch them and report back to you should they find anything."

"I look forward to hearing your reports, Matthew. Now I must leave you, for to be seen with you could compromise our roles. I bid you farewell for now." He stood, gave a small priestly bow to them all, and left.

Alexa looked up. "That was short and sweet. Let's head for the Basilica and there we must separate. Hats cannot be worn in there, but as a woman I am allowed a veiled headscarf. That should be sufficient. Whatever we do, we should keep a distance from each other or there's just a chance we could be recognised."

There was no disagreement.

KEN FRY

Basilica Papale di Santa Maria Maggiore

The air inside was cool and refreshing and just the way to escape the humidity of the city of Rome. Bella and her three colleagues gulped in lungfuls of chilled air as they gazed around at the grandeur of the place. It was awash with works of art and sculptures that seemed to be in every corner or archway.

Kristy explained, "This is a major papal basilica and one of the Seven Pilgrim Churches of Rome, and it is the largest Marian church in Rome. There has been, it is said, a church on this site since the third or fourth century. Now look at it. Come on, Torriti's painting should be in the nave area."

The building was bigger than they had imagined but they reached the location after a brisk walk.

The painting had no significant placement, and many would have barely noticed it. A small group of people was also looking at it. There was one woman with them, wearing a veiled headscarf.

Max whispered, "That's hardly going to set the world alight, is it?"

"No, it's not," Kristy whispered back. "But just see what is going on there."

"What do you see?"

"A woman on her knees, dressed in a deep-red cloak of some sort offering a baby to a man who, without a doubt, is Jesus."

"Correct. Now, do you think this is his dying mother, Mary, offering her soul to him?"

"No way! That's hard to believe. Is this artist trying to tell us that the woman was handing him their baby?"

The veiled woman stepped back, her stiletto heel treading hard on his foot.

Max gave a short gasp of pain.

The woman turned her unrecognisable face to him. "*Signore, mi dispiace molto.*"

Max grimaced. "Think nothing of it." Pain momentarily went through all his toes and the rest of his foot.

The team seemed not to notice. They moved in for a closer inspection.

"It has a mosaic quality about it," Isabella noted.

"Apparently that was his trademark," Kristy replied. "What else do you notice?"

She carefully scanned the work. "Not much else. What's that red tower supposed to represent?"

"Like the colour red she wears, it has always been symbolic of the Magdalene."

As she spoke, unnoticed, the veiled woman moved away and came to stand behind them.

Kristy continued. "The tradition of painting her probably dates back to before the Renaissance era. She was, and still is, an intriguing figure for many artists. It seemed nobody could really make up their mind about her. She would be seen reclining on a bed after apparently giving birth to a baby and handing it to Jesus, who also holds another in his arms ... Their child, also? Hence, I guess, the term, 'Holy Family.'"

Not one of the team heard the low hiss that came from behind them. Nor did they feel or notice a scalpel blade swiftly and deftly slicing a small slit through the backpacks they were carrying.

Kristy continued. "All of you, look more closely at the

tiny, almost unreadable signature in the lower-left corner. What else do you see?"

Max produced his loupe and bent low for a closer inspection. "Bloody hell! I can see what you mean. It's a small, red, Templar-like cross."

They all took turns to examine it.

"Undoubtedly," Isabella stated, "there's something going on here. We don't know what, but if this doesn't give us a hint, I don't know what else will."

Kristy pointed to the figure of the woman handing over the baby to the white-robed figure of Jesus. "This is almost identical in every way to the fresco that can be found in Tempio Ormelle on the wall of a twelfth-century Templar church, Chiesa San Giovanni Battista dei Templari. It has been said by some that the Templars dedicated this church to their patron saint, the Magdalene – as the art so strongly suggests – and *not* the Virgin Mary. The sheer presence of the robe and the tower, I think, are indisputable evidence of that."

"We must see this. Jake, keep taking all the photos you can. So, how far from here is it, Kristy?"

"It's not far from Venice, about three hundred and fifty miles from here. Let me show you. I have a map here." She swung her backpack to her front, ready to open it, and let out a small cry. "What the hell has happened here?" Her expression was of puzzled concern. A neat horizontal slash ran through the fabric. "I've been robbed!" After a quick rummage through the contents, nothing she could see had been taken.

The others experienced the same thing with increasing alarm. Nothing had been taken.

"Just where and how did this happen?" Max asked as the others all looked shaken and shocked. "It must have been

THE MAGDALENE MISSION

done either on our journey here or when we stood in a group. It's the same sort of thing that happened to our luggage. Our stalker is still with us. Whoever it is seems to know every move we make."

"Who the hell can it be? I saw and felt nothing." Isabella scanned in every direction.

"Wait a minute." Max wrinkled his brow. "That woman who stepped hard on my toes, where did she go?"

"She left, so it couldn't be her. Did any of us get a good look at her?"

Jake answered, "No chance of that. She was heavily veiled."

"That sounds a bit too convenient. She seems to be the only one I had any contact with."

"Let's get out of here and head back to the hotel. Your comment, Kristy, on the name of the hotel could be true! We'll hire a car tomorrow and take that trip north. And remember, when we're back in our rooms, we won't mention what we're doing or where we're going."

🌹

Much later, Croxley, Alexa, and Bull sat at a pavement café together. Croxley was on the phone with Bishop Ignatius, discussing the events of that day. Alexa's role received special consideration and praise.

"Do you think I've driven them off?" she asked.

"Only time will give us an answer to that, but as I've said before, I would prefer it if they found what they are looking for. If they did that, we could destroy it totally. The last thing we want is for it to end up in some museum for all to see. I'm sure our bishop would agree with that. Is that not so, Bishop?"

The phone was on speaker. "Correct. Should they be driven off, that would be the least-successful result, for others will surely follow. Overriding all these considerations is the high possibility the missing codex does not even exist."

"What do you want me to do?" Bull sounded impatient. "The less flying I have to do, the better."

"Bull, I guessed as much. I sense your frustration. Take note of what the bishop has just said. Your turn starts tomorrow. They don't know who you are unless they recognise you from the other hotel. Bang off a few rounds just to keep them on their toes but aim to miss. I tell you this – if either of you two harm them in any way at this point, until I tell you to do so, I will abandon you. Is that understood?"

Two heads nodded in mutual agreement.

Chapter 20

The Following Morning

The team committed to a very early start in their hired vehicle, a classic Lancia Volumex VX Coupe. It was cramped for the backseat passengers but a thrilling and speedy drive. Max knew how to choose his cars. The journey was just over five hours, which included a few stops. Max, with the same heightened sense of security as all the others, forever checked his mirrors.

Something had caught his attention a while back.

"Don't want to worry you all, but somebody seems to have been following us for some distance. Whenever we pull over, so do they. Take a look."

They turned.

All they could see was a set of lights on a moving car behind them at some distance.

"Watch this." Max drove to the far end of a pull over and the set of lights following them did the same. "See what I mean?"

"It seems more than coincidence." Jake looked at the others. "What do you think?"

Isabella answered, "There's nothing we can do about it, but at least we have a visual to keep our eyes on. Let's get moving, eh?"

They continued on the long journey with the other car always at a reasonable distance behind. Max kept a wary lookout in his rear-view mirror and told the others not to look back so as to possibly alert the unknown driver that he had been spotted. Eventually, they followed the road signs to Tempio Ormelle. Another prominent road sign indicated, *La Chiesa di San Giovanni Battista*. The twelfth-century church stood in a prominent position and could not be missed.

There was comprehensive agreement that it was a beautiful building and that it had lasted so long was amazing. For a moment their pursuer was forgotten as they alighted and walked toward it.

"Oh my," Isabella whispered, "it's so beautiful."

A small cloister ran around the outside walls.

"The love and devotion that must have inspired this is still here and the entire building seems suffused with it," Kristy added.

Jake shook his head. "And so is our stalker. Don't turn around, but I've just seen him. White suit, Panama hat, and dark shades. Just be alert without being obvious."

Kristy seemed not to hear. Art, her beloved subject, took precedence. "Around the cloisters there are many frescoes. Most have faded, but just wait until you see Magdalene."

Halfway down, it could not be missed. The colours were as fresh as if it had been painted just a week ago. In form and construction, it was only a little different from the work in Rome. It was almost identical, but without the mosaic quality of its Roman counterpart.

"This is unbelievable." Max let his jaw hang open. "Why

hasn't it faded?"

"Nobody has an answer for that. It has been examined time after time, over and over again, and nobody can figure its condition out. It's a riddle, and many mystics have had a field day with suggestions of miraculous goings-on and all that. There's no signature, only the tiny Templar emblem in the bottom right-hand corner. There she is offering Jesus her child – or is it *their* child? There's also a tower standing nearby."

"Well, she must certainly be the child's mother," Max agreed.

"As I said before, just because an artist depicts it so doesn't mean it is the truth, does it?" Kristy reminded him. "You said there was no signature, and one would think you and the others who have examined it are correct."

In the corner, surrounded by green undergrowth, stood a tiny red Templar cross, similar to the Roman version.

Using his loupe, Max knelt in close and examined it. Several minutes later, he stood and gave a low whistle. "You're not going to believe this."

"Well, come on, tell us what you have found," Kristy prompted him.

"That miniature red cross, covered and surrounded with grass, weeds, and undergrowth, has a name on it. It's small and blends in with the grassy ambience. We've seen it the other day at the excavation site on that rusty sword. It's Percy de Havilland."

Their initial reaction was a stunned, astonished silence, followed by gasps of incredulity.

"It can't be!" Isabella exclaimed. "All this time, it has been here. Then you come and in five minutes, you find something that no other person, across *centuries*, has ever found. Let me look." She took the loupe and began to search. "I can't really make anything out apart from what looks like a 'd' and a capital 'H.' Just a mass of straggly grass, and certainly not his name."

"Let me look. I might be able to do better." Kristy took the loupe. She spent the same time examining it. "Yes! Yes, I can make out the name Percy, just. That's unbelievable." Her excitement was obvious.

Jake was next, but not before attaching close-up and micro lenses to his cameras and taking several shots. "No doubt about it. Max is right. If we hadn't seen that signature at the excavation site, we wouldn't have made this connection."

"Okay, I agree." Isabella looked at them. "What does this tell us? We need to discuss and evaluate this find and all its implications. Use all your equipment, Jake, and spare nothing. We had better head back and see what we can find out about our mysterious knight."

In their excitement, all thoughts of their stalker had been forgotten. That was until they became aware of him standing only five yards behind them. He was still wearing his large Panama hat and equally large dark glasses. His arms were folded across his chest. He was virtually unrecognisable and so confident that they had no idea he had been following them all the way from Rome.

Isabella saw him first and gave an audible gasp, her hand quickly covering her mouth. "Oh my God!"

The others swung around with startled apprehension.

Max moved forward, knowing it was not a time to make any unwise moves. "You startled us. Can we help you?"

"I don't think so." A faint smirk crossed his face. "You seemed so excited, I thought I'd see why." His mixed Bronx

THE MAGDALENE MISSION

and Italian accent were immediately noticeable to them.

"We have nothing to tell you. Just look for yourself if you're that interested." Isabella was unable to disguise the hostility in her voice, and try as she and the others might, she was unable to discern the man's features.

"Let's get out of here, team. We have a long trip back and more work to do." Max commanded.

Bull Morello bent low to look at the work but didn't really know what he was looking for. The rear tyre he'd punctured with a single muffled shot would give them some well-deserved aggravation.

It was several minutes later when the team arrived back at their vehicle. At first, they didn't notice anything. Jake spotted it first. The car had a slight lean to it, and he guessed it could mean only one thing – they had a flat back tyre.

"Oh, Jesus, look at that." He pointed to the shredded-looking back wheel with a neat but substantial hole on display.

"Shit!" Max looked angry. "It wasn't like that when we got here. It was perfectly okay." He peered down at the hole. "That was no stone or road debris. It looks more like a gunshot. Take a good look, everybody."

"I see what you mean, but how?" Isabella had a moment of realisation and gasped. "Oh no! What am I thinking?"

"I don't think there can be much doubt about that." Max sounded querulous. "We are not hanging around to find out. Jake, help me change this wheel and let's get out of here as fast as possible."

They set to it, working at speed. Bull Morello sauntered past them and without a second glance, clambered into his own vehicle and drove off. But not before giving a short, loud blast on the car horn.

"It had to be him!" Kristy shouted. "Did anyone get a good look?"

"Not much. I wouldn't be able to recognise him even if I saw him," Max told her.

"Well, we heard his odd American accent, and we know he's most certainly one of them, if there's more than one."

Jake hauled out the spare wheel and in no time, they were on their way again. There was no sign of the other car, and it was a long journey back.

Bull Morello felt pleased at his restraint and obeying his orders. He felt a glow of pride as Croxley congratulated him on his handiwork. His only regret was that he wished he could have gone further and smashed their faces in. "Boss, it could have all been over. There was nobody around and they would have left this world without witnesses."

"Not yet. You know we want to see what they find. Now, what were they getting excited about?"

"Some crappy old painting they kept peering at... and peering very hard."

"What was it? Do you know?"

"It was religious, with Jesus being handed a baby by a woman dressed in red. They took lots of photos of it."

Croxley's interest multiplied. "Magdalene, that's for sure! They are on to something. I'd love to see it. Let's hope they leave a camera around. It will be a job for Alexa. We also need to know what their next move will be. Alexa is going to be busy. She installed other bugs in their rooms, but they are not giving much away. They now know that we could be on to them. It's time to up the ante, so let the games begin."

Chapter 21

Two Days Later

Jake and Kristy had been busy with their photographs and those with the close-up macro lenses revealed clearly what Max had first seen. He printed out the most relevant. The long-lost signature was now more apparent, but still required close examination to reveal its entirety. Bella and Max were going through ancestry records back into the earliest available, those sparse and scarce medieval lineages. Some were in Jerusalem, France, Portugal, and England. It was painstaking work.

"Our Percy de Havilland must have had a high rank. Having his name engraved on his sword is indicative of nobility of some sort. Was he the artist of that painting? If so, it is even more remarkable," Max told them. "There were three main ranks in the Knights Templar – noble knights, sergeants, and chaplains. Only those from noble families whose fathers and grandfathers were knights could become noble knights. The sergeants were drawn from non-noble families and wore black or brown. Our Mr de Havilland is a mystery so far."

Bella agreed. "But how and why does he appear on a

THE MAGDALENE MISSION

medieval painting, and was there a connection between him and the past lineage of the Magdalene?"

"That is, I fear, impossible to find out. His devotion shines like the sun. Whatever happened to him? Does he have a connection with the casket we hope to find?" Max asked.

"I like to think he is heavily involved in it. It almost seems like we have been deliberately and mysteriously led along this route. Long may it continue."

The hours passed by before Isabella spoke. "I've been going through ancestry records both in the UK and France. Those of importance, it seems, are stored in national museums like the French Musée du Louvre or the British Museum. The name de Havilland is not common, but there are several to be found in the Louvre. These are interesting because some go back to the twelfth century, all the way through to the fifteenth century where, for some reason, they seem to stop. I think the extermination and dissolution of the Templars had much to do with that. It also lists their later wives, with the principal names being Francette, Marion, Audrey, Arienne, Reneé, and Perenelle. Now, Percy lived for certain in the thirteenth and fourteenth centuries, and that means we can rule out the later names like Francette, Audrey, and Arienne. That leaves us with Marion, Reneé, and Perenelle. All three are likely contenders to be married to our historic Percy de Havilland. Lo and behold, the records, dim and faded as they are, clearly show Marion as his wife. Not only that, alongside her name is a red Templar cross! This has to be the clue we are looking for. It appears she was married in Lyon, but when the dissolution came about via the Pope and King Philip of France, she and Percy, soon after the death of Jacques de Molay on the River Seine, fled to Tomar in Portugal, and with them, I am certain, went the casket containing de Molay's perfectly preserved heart. It states clearly on the documents, '… et il a emporté avec lui l'amour sans fin et le cœur de Jacques de Molay.' This means, '… and he did carry with him the never-ending love and the heart of Jacques de Molay." She paused and looked at their stunned expressions.

"That's an astonishing find, Bella. It's hard to believe." Max was wide eyed.

Jake added, "I know Tomar in Portugal. There's only one place they could have gone to, and that's the twelfth-century castle the Templars had built for their protection and safety. It's known as the *Convent of Christ Castle*. It's a well-visited tourist attraction because of its age and history with the Templars. I'm all for going there. It seems it has to be our next stop. I feel we are being guided. What do you all think?"

There was complete agreement and the listening devices planted around the rooms missed not a detail of their conversation.

The following day, they were booked in on the three-hour afternoon flight to Lisbon, which is roughly seventy miles from Tomar. They had also booked a car from the Lisbon airport. Max had made reservations at the Thomar Boutique Hotel, which was in easy reach of the castle. It seemed the perfect choice. They truly believed they had shaken off their stalkers.

Croxley was not bothered. He knew they were heading for Lisbon. They would be easy to find. Unbeknown to Isabella, Alexa had concealed a high-powered, wafer-thin GPS tracking device in the folds of her suitcase. It had a global tracking capability. Once in Tomar, there would be little trouble in tracking them, or anywhere else. All they had to do was watch and wait to see what they could find and then decide what to do next.

Their flight was uneventful and as much as Isabella looked around at the half-empty plane, no one looked suspicious.

"I think we may have shaken them off," Jake ventured.

"You've said that every time, and every time… you have been wrong," Kristy responded.

"Well, look around. Who do you suspect?"

"Whoever they are, we have always underestimated them and I'm not making that mistake again, nor should any of us."

"You're right, Kristy." Bella held her arm. "I've had enough scares to tell me you are right. Whatever we do, we have to be vigilant and alert about everything. This quest should be paying danger money."

The journey to Tomar went smoothly, with no following vehicle tracking them. They were forever checking, but there was nothing to see or to suspect. Approaching the city, the castle was clearly visible, as was its circular construction, in true Templar style.

Convent of Christ | Tomar, Portugal

"Wow!" Max was impressed. "That's what I call a castle. It reminds me a lot of the Templar church we saw in Tempio Ormelle. It looks like the same person has designed them both, except this is on a far larger scale. There must be a connection. I can't wait to get inside tomorrow."

Bella sounded excited. "Me too, but we don't know what we are looking for. There must be something in there that could give us a clue of some sort, surely? Find the casket and I think we'll find her gospel. I think each of us should go through an allocated area inch by inch and see if there's anything we can come up with."

THE MAGDALENE MISSION

Croxley's flight was some hours behind his quarry, but he had booked a car to Tomar. There was little doubt they would find them quickly, and once on the outskirts, the GPS was activated by remote control, and they'd know precisely where they were.

They headed towards the signal. It was being emitted from the Thomar Boutique Hotel. Alexa was already using one of her passports under a different name and a disguise to match. She was unrecognisable. Checking in was not a problem.

Chapter 22

By ten-thirty the next morning, Bella and her team were inside the holiest section of the castle – the circular part constructed by the Templars. They divided it into quarters between them. Armed with powerful flashlights, they proceeded to scour the walls, ceiling, and floor, inch by inch. Countless photographs using a variety of lenses were taken of anything that had relevance.

The hours passed by.

Nothing.

They returned to their hotel, unaware their rooms had been bugged.

They spent considerable time going through each shot they'd taken.

Kristy broke the spell with an excited yell. "I don't believe this!"

"What?" They all shouted at once.

"Listen, all of you, to what I'm about to say. I can hardly believe it, but it is written here in the lingua franca of the time, French, when English was not in use. I am literally shaking, almost in disbelief. When I translate what is written, it reads

THE MAGDALENE MISSION

in the English that we use today, which was not known in those days." She began to sob.

Bella moved to her and placed her arm around her. "Kristy, what have you found? Tell us, please."

"Okay." She stifled a sob. "Here it is."

The heart and words that you seek
Are laid to rest
In a land of mystique,
Albion.
In its soil
So blessed
His heart doth beat
Beloved home of Marion
Safe and sure from defeat.'

Kristy, wiping away tears, read it out loud three more times.

Not a word was spoken.

Profound silence.

Max, Bella, and Jake rushed across to her table to examine in close detail what she had discovered. Sure enough, it was as she said.

"This cannot be real." Isabella was shaking. "But it *is* real. A verse, centuries old, written in medieval French, that when translated, becomes a rhyming modern-style English verse."

"It's real, all right. It mentions Marion – could that be Percy's wife, or could it mean the Magdalene? Why has this never come to light, after all this time?" Max looked aghast. "Also, who wrote it? It looks as if it was meant for us and has been waiting here so long for us to find it. We have been led here, it seems. Now I'm being stupid."

"No, you're not, Max. I think you're right. Probably its small size, and the fact that it's situated at the top of a tall column, is why it has been missed." Kristy had regained her composure. "It's like it's been sitting there just waiting for us to appear with an honest and sincere agenda. But that seems far too fanciful."

"One thing's for certain," Max said. "We have no choice but to do as it asks, no matter how weird and strange it may seem. Albion was the earliest-known name for the island of Britain. It was used by ancient Greek geographers from the fourth century B.C. and even earlier, who distinguished 'Albion' from smaller members of the British Isles. The Greeks and Romans probably received the name from the Gauls or the Celts."

"So where did Marion come from? France, Portugal, or Britain?"

"It specifically says Albion, and that's clear. We need to know who Marion refers to and why it should be Britain. What nationality was she and was she married to Percy de Havilland, which seems to be the case so far? Another thing, was de Havilland an English or French knight? Most of the knights after the Norman invasion were French. The British aristocracy is riddled with French names and ancestry, like Fitzwilliam, Mayhew, d'Arcy, and Martin."

"As we are in Portugal, we had best start here, checking what records we can. So, let's spread out around this building and leave no brick untouched as far as we can," Kristy suggested.

Isabella headed for the cloisters, of which there were eight. The one that interested her most was the Claustro do Cemitério, the Cloister of the Cemetery. It was the burial site for monks and knights of the order. Whilst it was built after

THE MAGDALENE MISSION

de Havilland's period, it was known that earlier tombs and records to be interred there. For many, it was a spiritual and mystical place. That observation became real the more she scoured it inch by inch. The entire structure had an aura of sacredness about it, but there was nothing to be found, nothing that could be linked to de Havilland. Her understanding of the Portuguese language was limited, but she was basically capable.

It was then that she came across what looked like a plain, unnamed tomb. Its only marking was a clearly defined sword bearing an engraved Templar icon. As it was a Templar building, there was no surprise in that. A close inspection revealed an inscription woven along the blade and around the hilt. Bending closer, she took several shots of it. Using her lens, she began to read it. Several minutes later, she took a step backwards and at the same time, took a deep breath before sharply exhaling. She wrote down what she had made of it. It did not rhyme, verse-like, as the other, but the words were even more startling.

> *Sir Percy doth rest here in peace, from our sacred walls now long departed. His beloved troth, brave Marion, flies back to her blessed Isle of Albion. Carries she his golden coffer to a long dead King, the living heart of our Master Grand to offer, and the words of our cherished Saint Magda, to be safe until the end of days.*

A sense of shock pulsated through her. Several seconds passed before a loud, unstoppable whoop burst from her wide-open mouth. Turning, she ran to find the others. They had all heard the shout and rushed towards her. Her words came out in a scrambled torrent of amazed virtual disbelief.

In minutes, they were all gathered around the stone construction as she translated what she had found and read.

"That answers a whole load of questions, I think." Max looked astonished. "C'mon, let's get out of here and find a quiet bar where we can talk this over. These have to be incredible finds and confirmation of what we are trying to locate. This is unbelievable!"

A bar was soon found. No one spotted a man, all in black, with a woman dressed in a nurse's uniform holding his arm, following a short distance behind them.

The team sat at a table near the bar, ordered their drinks, and began to discuss Bella's findings.

The couple walking behind them sat close by and they could see and tell by the team's body language and excited voices that they had found something of importance. They sat quietly and said nothing. This was just the thing Croxley and Bishop Ignatius would be anxious to hear about.

"That's bloody amazing, Bella. Proof positive, ninety-nine per cent, but what does it all mean?" Jake looked excited.

Max responded, "It means the remains of Jacques de Molay, in a gold casket, are buried somewhere in Britain, together with the missing words of the Magdalene Gospel. That inscription clearly states that."

Kristy looked up. "A long-dead king. Who and what and where can that be? Britain has had dozens of them. Some genuine, some just the stuff of legends and nothing more. It would be helpful if we knew more about Marion, like who was she, where did she come from, and why offer de Molay's remains to a long-dead king? I don't get it."

"Well," said Bella, "it's obvious. If the Catholic Church and King Philip of France knew of it, whatever remains existed would be found and destroyed. The safest haven would, of

THE MAGDALENE MISSION

course, be Britain – or Albion, as the writer states. It also seems more than likely that Marion was from Britain, a land difficult to assault and with a formidable aggressive reputation."

"So… when do we leave and where do we go? This is an almost impossible task." Jake looked concerned.

Bella spoke. "Our mission has been clear and has taken us around the Middle East and a good chunk of Europe only to redirect us back to where we started from. We could not have known that. We now need to narrow down the long-lost and dead kings of England and see if we can, in some way, connect them with Marion. That's some task."

"Not that difficult," said Kristy. "From my past research studies, I have a list of them back home, at least seventy. Now, get this, I also happen to know where they were born, siblings, and where they are buried or supposed to be. They date from the fourth century up to the present day. They are all on my computer, and I can upload them to us here to search through. The first thing we do is dump King Arthur. There's no proof positive that he was real. More than likely, he was a myth, a legend. Before we start, he is eliminated."

Max gave her a hug. "That sure does take a lot of work away from us. Would we be able to track down a line from a king to the Middle Ages, and the ancestry?"

"Of course."

"So, if we find a Marion around the thirteenth or the fourteenth centuries, we can backtrack to the intended long-dead king?"

"Exactly."

"If we assume Percy was of aristocratic lineage, it becomes more likely that his Marion came from noble stock."

"Without a doubt. Peasants were kept at arm's length."

"Nothing new there, then," Jake quipped, causing smiles

from all. "Well, where do we start, Kristy?"

"If you all agree, I don't think we need go back before the seventh century, otherwise it is all too vague."

There was no dissent.

"This seems all so distant from our objective of finding the missing gospel parts," added Max.

"I agree," added Bella, "but it does seem very likely that de Molay, the casket, the Knights Templar and Mary's gospel are intertwined in a manner none of us ever could have imagined. What we discovered in India and the Tibetan monastery is compelling evidence that she wrote down or had written for her all she had heard and understood from Yeshua."

Bull Morello looked at Alexa and she nodded. His thoughts needed no explanation.

"Don't overdo it. Just a short, sharp reminder should be enough. This could be fun. Go to it."

Bull smirked, pushed back his chair, stood, turned, and began walking towards the seated four. He was not seen or noticed coming up from behind. Drawing as close as he dared, he appeared to trip and, in doing so, crashed heavily into their table, upsetting all their drinks before tumbling to the floor and letting out a sharp curse.

"Jesus!" shouted Max.

They all sprang to their feet with drinks spilt all over them.

Before they could move, the sprawling man was up on his feet and looking dangerously angry. He pointed at Max. "You stuck your foot out deliberately. I saw you."

"I beg your pardon?" Max looked startled.

"You heard me, Mac!" Bull clenched rock-hard fists.

"You must be mistaken. My foot was under this table."

"Bullshit, buddy!" He swung a punch at Max.

Max had seen it coming and stepped out of range, so the swing missed. "Hey, squire, there's no need for that, but if I was wrong, I apologise profoundly."

"You shit-faced Brits are all a bunch of MFs."

"No need for that, sir. Take it easy and please let me buy you a drink."

"Fuck your drink! You be careful. If I come across you again, you know what to expect." He turned and headed back to his table, now careful to keep a low profile.

Alexa stood up, took his arm, and steered him away to the exit.

Back at Bella's table there was an astonished silence, which Jake broke.

"Who the hell was that idiot?"

"No idea," said Max. "I've never seen him in my life before."

"I have." Bella looked around at them all. "I didn't recognise him, but that odd American accent was a giveaway. I'm certain it was the man in white we met the other day at Tempio Ormelle, although this time he is dressed in black. That sing-song accent was a dead giveaway. I'd put money on it. What do you think?"

"I think you are bang-on, Bella. If so, how would he know we are here?"

"I've no idea, but he does, and that's enough for me."

"Back to the UK, and fast, I say," Kristy said. "We have an abundance of clues and leads and we should turn up something, providing our stalkers can't find us."

"We are on the move once again, and I just hope it comes to something *before* our pursuers find us. We've survived them so far, so let's keep it that way. I can't understand what they are trying to do."

"Whoever it is," added Bella, "I am certain it has something to do with Magdalene's missing gospel pieces. They want to trash it in some way, should it be found. UK it is, then."

Chapter 23

Croxley was desperate to learn where they would be going in Britain, and as yet, had no idea. He had decided that, along with a disguised Alexa, he would track them closely himself. Morello, now recognisable, had to be out of sight, but close by and covered up, unrecognisable, ready to play his part should and when the going got tough. From the implanted bugs and listening device, it was discovered that they were catching the midday flight from Lisbon to Gatwick in the UK. From there, they were to make their way to the residence of the team member named Kristy.

Without a doubt, they had to be on the same plane or it was possible that they could lose the trail totally. There was no trouble in doing so. Bull, with his claustrophobia, was sat in a nearside window seat, his face partially covered with a scarf, so he was able to gaze out and not feel so trapped. Even that did not prevent his heart rate from increasing and sweat from dripping from every pore of his body. It was a long way to fall.

Alexa, disguised as an inconspicuous tourist with mousey

hair, a missing front tooth, large horn-rimmed glasses and again under a different passport name, sat on the outside seat, with Croxley seated centre. They had a clear view of Isabella and her companions. They were not recognised.

Isabella's gaze swept across the distant clouds. Radiant and forever rolling, they shone with the imitative splendour of lost treasures.

Thoughts of what might be encountered in their quest sent vibratory sensations through her mind, heart, and stomach.

A prayer, silent as the rising moon, passed through her tingling being.

Dear God, am I alone in these feelings? I hope not. Are we being guided? What we have been through has been extraordinary and dangerous. The whole thing has moved me. I am too shy to admit to the others such personal feelings. Grant us what we seek. Grant it for her, and for humanity.

Her tears flowed.

She wiped her eyes clear before the others could notice.

It was her first prayer since she was a questioning teenager, and she was not certain if she meant it in either a religious or adulatory fashion.

Kristy looked animated. "I think my research from back then is going to be useful. I already have a few ideas, but they could be wrong. We will soon find out."

The flight went smoothly, with no mishaps. In less than three hours, the plane landed safely at Gatwick. Four hours later, they were at Kristy's home, a large multi-bedroomed

THE MAGDALENE MISSION

Georgian structure set close to the village of Broadway in the Cotswolds, along a range of rolling hills that rose from the meadows of the upper Thames to an escarpment above the Severn Valley and Evesham Vale. It was an idyllic location and would be their HQ until they decided to make their exploratory trips. Unbeknown to them, their journey and destination was monitored. They thought that they were safe and had thrown off their stalkers.

The following day, Kristy appeared with two large laundry baskets filled with folders to the brim. Each was labelled with names and dates, some going back to the ninth century and up to the eighteenth century. She gave a pile to each of them. "We are looking for two names, Percy de Havilland and a woman who we only know as Marion. Some of these records go far back, and others not so far. Should we find anything, more than likely we will be able to trace back to the mysterious long-lost king. What I suggest is that Jake and I work forward from the ninth-century kings, noting if their burial whereabouts are known. I have a comprehensive record of these. Isabella, you, and Max start from the sixteenth century and work backwards to find as many likely candidates and siblings as possible around at the times you are looking at. That will be the difficult part, for there could be as many as eight, and each of those with just as many siblings. With luck, we will meet up in the middle."

Each pair took a basketful and started on the task.

Three hours later, Bishop Ignatius, sitting in his resplendent office decorated with paintings of saints and numerous crucifixes, received his requested Skype call from Croxley. He was not in a happy frame of mind. Never noted for his patience, Ignatius was experiencing a sharp rise in his blood pressure. He had been expecting faster results but as yet, nothing concrete had materialised from what remained a venture of considerable expense. To date, it had been nothing but journeys crisscrossing Europe, the Middle East, and Asia, all of which amounted to the total sum of zero for their endeavours. The researchers had not been frightened off. On the contrary, they appeared more determined in their quest. The scare tactics had clearly failed. He was beginning to think he had chosen the wrong person for the mission.

"Listen to me, Mr Croxley." The former, friendly 'Matthew' address had gone. "I am disappointed with your results so far. Have you no idea what they are up to and where they are going next? To date, you have been more than fortunate in managing to keep track of them and their activities. Do you truly understand what we have entrusted you with? Do you? What you are entrusted with is the preservation of Christianity, as we both understand it. So far, nothing has happened. I think that the time has come for a serious appraisal of tactics. In fact, I demand it."

Croxley saw the bishop's fist raise high and heard it come down hard on the tabletop. He began to speak "Easy, Bishop, easy, but—"

Ignatius cut him short. "What is it with you, Croxley? You joyride all over Europe and foreign lands and you have nothing to show for it. My patience is at an end. Get a substantial result or, if you can't, then just dispose of them as you know how and wish. You will receive no more funding unless we have a positive outcome by the next time I call. Do you understand me, Croxley? Have I made myself clear?"

"More than enough," Croxley answered, and for a rare moment in his life he felt inadequate. "But, Bishop, it seems they are on the verge of a major find. Shouldn't we wait to see what they find?"

"You heard what I said, Croxley. I couldn't be clearer and more precise. Just get on with it or the entire operation ceases." The bishop powered down the transmission without waiting to hear any more.

Croxley wriggled as the contents of his intestines did a dance routine through his pulsating bowels. The prospect of not receiving more money was nerve racking. There was no way that could be allowed.

Croxley was having a change of heart. Criminality had not entirely left him. He reasoned his church, doing God's work, could use such methods. His original plan to destroy any finds was placed on the back burner and needed to be revaluated.

Bishop or no Bishop, he hasn't a clue. I want to find what they are looking for as much as he does. If I must deceive him, then so be it. He wants them wasted if need be. Okay, but just not yet. I want to see what they find. I could make millions if I got my hands on it. No, no, no, my fat bishop. I am doing this my *way.*

He called Alexa and Bull Morello. They appeared in minutes.

"Look, you two, our bishop is getting impatient. He is not happy. He wants us to finish the job by possibly wasting our friends, if we have nothing to show for it. Otherwise, all future funding will cease. I don't agree. He has underestimated my abilities. I'm not so certain that we should wipe out these people. Just think of the money we would make if they found what they are looking for and we got our hands on it. It would be worth billions to the right buyer. We could all become multi-millionaires overnight – and I mean *multi*." Before they could protest, he added, "Just in case you are wondering, think of the good we could do through our church in furthering God's work. We wait until they find this Magdalene stuff and then we pounce. We have God on our side. I will keep the bishop happy and hanging on a string. We need his funding, so from now on, we do nothing but let our targets get on with their work and we keep silent watch. Alexa, your spying skills are very much needed here. Somehow, we have to bug that house. Can you do that without being discovered?"

Alexa's expression hardened. "Can a swan swim?" she retorted. "You should know by now, Matthew, you only have to ask and consider it done."

Croxley had his answer. He nodded. "When?"

"They have a habit of going for lunchtime drinks and eats. That's the best time. It will only take a short while to set up and we, from our hotel, should be able to hear what they are planning. When it is done, let me know where they are drinking and I will go alone, in disguise. You two would be in danger of being recognised."

"Agreed," he replied, "but the pair of you, no more scare tactics. Let them think they are safe and out of harm's way. Let them get on with it, and we will wait to see what they can come up with. If they find what they are looking for, it will be ours. Ignatius ... We will have to think about that. We have skills and weapons that should easily cause them to agree to our terms. They will have no chance, and with what I am now thinking and with the grace of the Almighty, we will be far richer, by the millions, each. That's somewhat better than his quarter-of-a-million offer. How does that sound? Just think how we could make our church a force to be reckoned with."

"I'll start right now." Alexa looked excited. "Whatever you do, don't go to the Lygon Arms. That's where they'll be. They are certainly not short of funds."

"Get to it, and let me know how it's going."

Bull Morello looked peeved. "I was expecting some action, but all we seem to do is sit around and wait."

"That, Bull, is about to change, believe me."

Chapter 24

Kristy and Jake began their search with King Egbert, a ninth-century monarch who died in 839.

Jake gasped. "I don't believe this. We have only just begun, and his remains are alleged to be in a mortuary casket with five others and get this, they can all be found in Winchester Cathedral. That's astonishing! Kristy, shouldn't we look at these first? It seems no coincidence that six long dead kings or high-ranking elites are buried in just what we are looking for... mortuary caskets in a great cathedral."

"Well, it's a start. Who are the others?"

"I'm not certain, but I know that Cnut the Great and William the Second are suspected of being in those caskets. Alfred's daughter Ælthryth of Wessex is known to have married Baldwin the Second of Flanders and was a countess who operated in Flanders and France. She had children, and there's a recorded link through an entire line of countesses and kings that goes well into the late Middle Ages and beyond. In a remote way, they are all linked to Ælthryth, daughter of King Alfred. Along the line, we find in the later

THE MAGDALENE MISSION

years that they had various children, and the family lines became very wide and confusing. There must be a Marion in there somewhere in the late thirteenth or early fourteenth centuries married to a French nobleman, Percy de Havilland. Remember, he was a Knight Templar, and Godfrey, a descendant of Baldwin, was at the time ruler of Jerusalem, and he was around at the time of de Molay's death in 1314." Jake was burning with curious enthusiasm.

Max and Bella joined in.

"So, in a distant way, he is linked to this puzzle?" Bella asked.

"Exactly. If we can find her name, it should be possible to link her back way into the earlier ages and find out which king it was about," Jake agreed.

Bella continued, "I think we are on the right path, but the only problem is that it was not uncommon for families to have five or six children and for each of *them*, in turn, to have the same number when they became married. There have to be hundreds to sift through, but our biggest clue is de Molay's death date."

"Well," said Max, "we need to put our emphasis on Percy's activities in the late thirteenth and early fourteenth centuries."

There was complete agreement and each concentrated on direct descendants of Baldwin, William, and Edward.

Bull Morello took stock of his growing frustration from sitting about not doing anything much. It was not what he had joined Croxley for. A more exciting panorama had been his expectation. A serious turn of events began formulating in his brain, perhaps another shooting or a kidnapping came quickly to mind – why not both? The kidnapping was dismissed as unworkable in their circumstances. A few shots would liven things up, somewhat irrespective of Croxley's directive. Besides, if he worked alone, nobody would know and there could be some fun to relieve the boredom. Disagreeably, the endless waiting aggravated his claustrophobia. That had to be handled.

Later that day, he skipped the hotel to work out how he was to do it. There was no way he wanted Croxley or Alexa to know what he had in mind. A few shots here and there would have an interesting effect.

First of all, the house would have to be looked at and people's movements checked. He didn't want to be seen by anybody, and that included Croxley and Alexa. There was no hurry, and she had first to put her listening devices in place. Once that was done, that would be the time to operate.

Kristy gasped excitedly. "Hey, I think I've found something!"

"What is it?" Isabella rushed over to her.

Both men stopped what they were doing and strode over to her. She was examining a fat file headed '100 years 1315-1415.' It was her synopsis of dates, names, places, marriages, births, and deaths of the early medieval French nobility, kings and queens and people of high rank. In it was her own commentary concerning the roles of important people and how they influenced the culture of the time.

"I've found this. Look!" Her finger jabbed at the page. "I've written in the English transcript. It reads that a certain Percy

THE MAGDALENE MISSION

de Havilland was distantly related to William le Marshal, First Earl of Pembroke, and did marry Marion of Flanders. Via Count Baldwin of Flanders, she has a traceable lineage back to King Alfred. That's it, that's our link. It lies with these two. They are distant heirs, and that Percy was a Templar narrows it down considerably. As we always suspected, the missing kings are Alfred, William, or Edward the Second, and it could be any of them. Alfred's tomb has never been truly found, William was interred in Westminster Abbey, and Edward – who was reigning when de Molay died – can be found at Gloucester Cathedral."

"But," said Max, "that inscription said long dead, but neither King William nor Edward were long dead. So where does that leave us?"

"A whole bunch of obscure eighth-to-tenth-century kings few have ever heard of." Jake shook his head.

Kristy got up to make coffee. Before she could begin pouring, there came a loud retort. The window overlooking the garden smashed into a shower of glass and the pot she was holding spilt like an earthquake crack, with hot coffee splattering everywhere. Her arms and shoulders began bleeding.

Astonished silence.

Before anyone could say or do anything, another explosion smashed a window, spattering more glass before a bullet embedded itself in a heavy oak cupboard.

Max yelled, "Down, everybody hit the floor! Stay flat. We are being attacked!"

No one needed a second warning. As they dove, yet another shot hit the room, quickly followed by another and another. The place was a mess of broken glass, porcelain, and blood from Kristy's wounds.

Max crawled out on his stomach to all the outer doors and slammed shut all the bolts and locks. He made it to the stairs before another shot splintered the banister he was about to grab. He crashed to the wooden flooring with his arms around his head.

All went quiet and not a sound was heard until Bella called out, "Max. Max, are you okay?"

From beneath his arms, he shouted back, "Yes, I'm okay, but stay down until I tell you to move."

For what seemed like an eternity, not a sound was heard until Max cautiously arose and, bending double, made it back to the living room. "You all okay here?"

Kristy replied, "Not me. I've been hit by flying glass. I am bleeding in a few places."

Max looked at her and she was shaking. "Holy shit! I thought we had made it away from these people."

Jake headed for the medical cabinet in the bathroom. He soon reappeared with bandages, tweezers to remove glass splinters, and plasters.

Isabella looked tentatively out of the intact window. There was nothing to be seen. Their assailant had vanished. "What do we do now?" She sounded shaken.

"We get the hell out of here as soon as we can. Somehow, these people seem to know everything we do. That casket must be somewhere around here, and these people want it! We have three possible destinations. Now we only discuss our movements in the car and nowhere else. We're being bugged. There's no other way they could have traced us here. In the morning, we leave, and once in the car, we discuss our plans."

There was no disagreement. The night was spent restlessly, with everyone on edge and awake before dawn broke.

THE MAGDALENE MISSION

Her long, pointed fingers activated the listening and recording devices she had installed in Kristy's home.

What Alexa heard startled her.

There was an on-going discussion concerning lineage and locality, which was abruptly broken up by the unmistakeable sounds of gunshots and vocal alarm. She needed no interpretation. It had to be Bull breaking his instructions. He was letting loose a volley of shots for whatever reason he had in his mind.

She, herself, was bored rigid and had sympathy for what he had done. Her inbred loyalty was to Croxley, her lifelong mentor, but this venture was like watching paint dry. She decided to say something, but only in private with Bull. Before she switched off, she did note that they would only make decisions within the car.

That would not do.

It had to be bugged, complete with a tracking device.

She decided to do that the same evening. The research team had no escape.

Chapter 25

The following morning, Kristy had a same-day replacement company fix the shattered windows the bullets had hit. Once the work was completed, they moved into the car to discuss their next move. They had decided not to call the police, as their main concern was to get away as fast as possible.

"The way I see it," said Bella, "is that we have a number of choices in different locations, and each with several contenders. These are New Minster, Hyde Abbey in Winchester – and also the cathedral there – Glastonbury Abbey, and Westminster. There are a few others, like the abbeys of Sherborne, Wimborne, and Shaftesbury. They all have potential."

"One thing is for certain," said Max, "we can't go digging up graves or breaking open church coffins, tombs, or caskets. We would be arrested. I am a qualified archaeologist and, with our joint credentials and sponsors, I'm sure we can find some leeway if we approach it correctly. What do you all think?"

Kristy was first to speak. Her arm and shoulder were

THE MAGDALENE MISSION

bandaged where Jake had picked out the glass fragments. "With what's happening around here, I'm not safe in my own home. It's time to get out of here and right now I don't care where we go."

"Let's do Sherborne." Max jabbed at his road map. "It's the least complicated and it has the grave of Æthelbald, who died in the ninth century. He was King of Wessex."

"But didn't he marry his stepmother, Judith, and wasn't she known to have had children?"

"That's why we should check him out first," Max said.

Kristy continued, "What exactly are we looking for?"

"No idea, but we've been lucky so far and found clues others have missed for centuries."

"Long may it continue!"

Their words came loud and clear. Her snooping device was behaving perfectly. She had no idea where the locations that they had mentioned were. That didn't matter – the tracking GPS she had attached under the back seat of their car, once activated, would take care of that problem.

Later that day, with a knowing look, she spoke directly with Bull. "You had some fun, then, yesterday?"

His expression was blank. "I don't know what you mean."

"Oh, I think you do. My equipment picked up every noise – shouts and gunshots."

A look of caution crossed his face. "I was bored."

"I envy you. I just wish I could have been with you, and don't worry, I won't say a word to Matthew. But next time you decide on something like that, you include me and not a word will reach him."

"Thanks. I promise."

"Better come with me now. I'm reporting back to him about what they are planning, and it looks like we have more travelling to do, but don't worry, it's all by road."

In ten minutes, they were with Croxley, and she gave her report.

A thoughtful look passed over his face. "It's in your hands. You have the knowledge, and we will follow you on this. There's no need for us to be in visual contact, your tracker takes care of that. We won't be seen, no danger of it. Whatever they do, let them get on with it – and no rough stuff."

Alexa gave Bull a knowing glance.

His expression remained blank.

The following morning, after breakfast, Max elected to drive. He had decided on using the M5 motorway. The journey was two and a half hours long. They were especially cautious when they stepped out of the car. Each scanned around in all directions. They didn't see anything. All was clear, yet throughout the journey they constantly checked behind them. There was nothing suspicious. They were not being followed.

After a stop for a short break, they arrived in sight of the abbey. Their fears were forgotten as they gazed at the handsome building. It was a mixture of construction styles – Saxon, Norman, and Early English.

"Smart gaff," muttered Jake. "What are we looking for, and where?"

Kristy answered, "We have one objective. There are two

THE MAGDALENE MISSION

kings entombed here, so the experts think. They are Æthelbald, King of Wessex, and his brother, also a king of Wessex, Æthelberth. The important thing to note is that they were both older brothers of King Alfred the Great."

"Okay, so where do we look?"

"They lie together in the north choir aisle. Let's get going!"

Once inside, the vaulted ceilings were breathtakingly impressive. They resisted the distraction and headed directly to the north choir aisle. Without realising it, they almost passed the tombs. They were small and virtually lost in the surrounding magnificence.

"Hold it!" Kristy shouted. "This is it."

They came to an abrupt halt only to gaze on two insignificant-looking tombs complete with modern-day biographies implanted on metal stands before each.

Bella read them aloud. "Well, they tell us nothing we didn't know before. Are these of any use to us?"

"None whatsoever." Max spoke. "This place was started at the beginning of the eighth century and hardly anything is known about these two, apart from that which is recorded by Bishop Asser of Sherborn of the period, who also wrote the biography of King Alfred. Not much to go on. Let's scour them with our lenses. Take as long as you like, and we might find a clue or two."

"Let's do it. Two of us on each." Bella knelt to start looking from the very bottom of the stone coffin.

Outside in the car park were several cars. A new camper wagon pulled in before gently coming to a stop.

Inch by inch, they minutely examined the coffins. Jake, using various close-up lenses, took photographs of anything on them that could be of interest. Some of the ancient graffiti went back to the Norman times and early Middle Ages. Time had rendered many of them unreadable. What examples were decipherable would have to be individually examined in detail before they moved on to other sites.

"I've found nothing of interest that gives a hint or clue about Marion, the Templars, or the Magdalene." Isabella gave a large sigh.

"Nor have we." Kristy sounded disappointed.

"What we have found has to be finely checked and examined. We can't go anywhere else until that's done." Max stood and looked around. "I suspect that's all we are going to find in this place, but let's do a quick tour anyway before we head back."

They all agreed, and they began a slow walk around the structure. The abbey was a popular place for visitors and there were many about. There was little for them to latch on to. Walking behind them, unnoticed, was an aged nun with a slight stoop and wearing a hearing aid. Where they stopped, so did she. There was a rosary wrapped around her wrist and she clutched what appeared to be a small prayer book. Every so often she would kneel for a short prayer.

The team carefully examined every wall plaque, inscription, and religious object, but to no avail.

"I think we have done enough here. There seems nothing we can link in with Marion or the casket. Let's get back and check the photographs," Jake suggested.

They turned around, narrowly missing a collision with the closely following nun.

"Oh, I'm so sorry," said Jake. "We didn't see you."

"Think nothing of it," muttered the nun with her head bent low.

Nothing more was said as they headed for the exit. They didn't see the nun straighten and speak into her prayer book, which contained a disguised GPS mobile device.

Reaching the exit, they strode out into the sunshine.

"Why is it whenever we go somewhere," said Kristy, "there's always someone close behind us?"

"I was thinking the same thing." Bella looked concerned. "Are you thinking what I am thinking or are we getting too jumpy?"

Max spoke. "Have you noticed? Whenever we're all together at meals, there's always a woman sitting near us, on a cell phone."

"Now that you mention it," Jake stared around, "it reminds me of that woman I saw on the plane when we first started out on this. But what we just encountered was a nun, not a pistol-packing lunatic. Hey, what am I thinking?"

"Well, let's see tonight. On the way back, let's decide if there's anything positive from Jake's photographs to decide where we go next." Isabella opened the car door, and they bundled inside.

Chapter 26

They began a careful examination of all their notes and Jake's photographs when they arrived back at the hotel bar before dinner. As amusing and interesting as many were, there was only one, an image of an etching on Æthelbald's tomb, that had a vague ring of significance to it. It was dated, as far as could be deciphered, *'Thirteen-Twenty.'* It simply read, *'She has come.'* As tempting as it seemed, they were scholars and fanciful interpretations were always dismissed when lacking any proof.

Tempting.

Apart from that tantalising snippet, there was nothing that they could find that had any direct reference to Marion, the Templars, or the Magdalene.

"Well, that was a washout, apart from that small crumb of interest. It doesn't help us at all." Max sounded irritated.

"Well, where do we go next?" Isabella asked.

"We have several locations to choose from," Kristy replied. "Why not Wimborne Minster? Æthelred the First, another Wessex king who died in the later ninth century, is interred there. When he went, his younger brother Alfred the Great succeeded—"

Max interrupted. "I'll tell you where we need to go next, and that's into the dining room for dinner. C'mon, let's go and see if any lone female is sitting close by."

That raised a round of laughter. Quickly finishing their drinks, they headed for the dining room.

Minutes later, they were seated at their table with starched linen tablecloths and sparkling cutlery. They surveyed the room. They had it to themselves, and there was not a lone woman to be seen. They felt safe to talk.

"No mysterious nuns around," quipped Jake. "I was hoping I could get a good look and make some sort of connection."

"Perhaps we were wrong and have all become hyper jumpy." Bella looked around.

"Well, we have had enough reason to be." Max didn't look amused. "Whoever has been doing this to us, they have now upped their game and their attacks have now become serious and murderous in their intensity. We have every reason to be highly suspicious of anybody close to us. So, let's not forget that and be ever on high alert." He gestured with open hands.

"I agree. Don't forget, all of you, I practically got in front of a bullet." Kristy wasn't smiling.

"You're right," said Max, "And so did I, out in your hallway. I'm not dropping my guard for one second."

They all agreed, and the discussion flipped to Wimborne Minster. They carried on, unaware of the small listening device adhered to the bottom of their reserved table.

Alexa made a note, *Wimborne Minster*, and again had no idea where it was. She also realised that now they were wary. She would have to change her tactics and resort to something less obvious. Meanwhile, the listening devices and tracker were doing an excellent job and could be relied on. She decided she would tell Croxley where they were heading next, and then go to the dining room, but sit nowhere near them and keep away from her cell phone. Another change of outfits was called for.

Entering the dining room just behind them, she made certain her table was well away from theirs, and she sat with her back to them. Her earpiece was firmly in place, and she wouldn't miss any part of their conversation. Wearing a heavy tweed skirt, a jumper, cardigan, and flat shoes, her wardrobe was academic, complemented by rimless pince-nez glasses and a thick volume of Russian literary novels. She could have stepped out of any university in the world.

In spite of their professed vigilance, the team barely gave her a second glance. She seemed unimportant. The disguise was perfect.

Jake dismissed any idea of her being a suspect – she wasn't close to them nor facing them. Scanning the other diners, he found nothing that raised any alarms.

They each took turns following his example, and they all came up with nothing.

"Let's talk freely." Bella guessed they were safe from being overheard. "We now know Marion of Flanders was married to de Havilland and that she had a direct link to Count Baldwin by Judith of Wessex, who had links with Alfred the Great. To me, it is possible she could have buried that casket with any of three or four kings – Alfred, Eadred, Edward the Elder, or Edmund. All were related to Alfred the Great in

THE MAGDALENE MISSION

some way. To me, it seems natural she would bury the casket near a king who was in some way related to her."

"The problem is Alfred's tomb has never been found, so we have three positive searches. I'm still intrigued by that early medieval graffiti … *She has come*."

"As it is, it's meaningless." Max never liked speculative research.

Bella responded, "Well, I have a feeling we are going to find out sooner than we think. A woman's intuition, you might say."

Kristy joined in. "I think Bella is right. Our next visit must be to the closest site to us here, which is Glastonbury Abbey, now an archaeological ruin. When that's done, we can then go on to Winchester."

"Who is at Glastonbury?" Max asked.

"There were two, Edmund and Edgar, both tenth-century monarchs. There was a third, Edward the Martyr, but his remains are now enshrined and rest in a Greek Orthodox church bearing his name in Brookwood Surrey. They were moved in 1988."

"Shouldn't we be looking at that too?"

"Yes, of course, but it's some distance from here."

"What do we know about these two?"

"There's not much we need to know. They were both related, as descendants of Alfred, and therefore Marion herself was a distant descendant. That's about all we can do right now, so let's set off tomorrow morning and see if there are more tantalising inscriptions waiting for us to find them!"

The following morning, they arrived at the ruined Glastonbury Abbey. It glistened in the well-manicured upkeep of its timeless decay. It had been destroyed by fire in the late twelfth century and rebuilding had immediately commenced.

Kristy told them what she knew. "Many of the burial spots were damaged or destroyed but they restarted the excavations. They were reburied or restored to their final resting places. Edmund's reign only lasted six months, so I think it unlikely we will find anything of interest there. Except maybe Edgar. He had his own chapel here, although not much remains of it. Disregard the spot where King Arthur and Queen Guinevere were supposed to be buried. That's a legend to encourage visitors."

The sun shone warmly on the ancient but broken structures. They were meandering around the crumbling stones when Kristy saw what they were looking for.

"Look, there it is. St Edgar and St Mary's Chapel." She pointed out what undoubtedly must have been an impressive construction in its time. What remained still, to this day, retained an imposing and elegant aura worthy of a king.

Moving closer allowed Jake to get to work with the camera. The nearer they got, the sharper it became.

"Wow." Bella was impressed. "To think, after all these centuries, it still retains an ancient grandeur."

"It's not huge, and the four of us should be able to cover its entirety in one long sweep. Let's go!" Max produced his loupe. "And don't dismiss anything as being as trivial as it might seem."

There was a period of silence broken only by the click of Jake's camera. As at Wimborne, there was graffiti spanning the centuries. There was nothing of any real significance.

THE MAGDALENE MISSION

Isabella then saw something that caught her eye, etched into the chest of a figure of a standing angel. It was a faint but discernible medieval inscription with raised letters and the figure of a female holding what looked like a Templar cross. With an excited shout, she called the others. "Look, look, this is riveting." She traced the letters with her finger. "And if that isn't a Templar cross, then I'm not Professor Isabella Vanton. What does it say, Max?"

Using his loupe, Max spent a short time examining it. "You are right, it is an early medieval inscription, and it is in Latin." Max adjusted his glasses. "It reads, 'Et manet. A verus cor non est inventus hic ire longius et ut inveniam.' That means, 'She awaits. A true heart is not found here. Go further and you may find.'"

"Oh my God!" A joint exclamation came from four mouths.

Bella became emotional. "That has been there for centuries, waiting for us to find it." Her eyes filled with tears. "This is just not possible, is it? Who wrote this, depicting a Templar Cross and a clear reference to a heart? It could be no other than Marion, could it?"

"It could be anybody." Max's usual dislike of speculative, non-scientific approaches showed. "I do concede, however, it is a massive indicator that further research is required. Where do we go from here?" He looked at Kristy.

She paused for a moment. "There are only two places I can suggest – Winchester and then Brookwood. There has to be a clue somewhere there, otherwise we'll come to a stop."

"We are not funded to come to a stop. We have to go on, no matter how long it takes. The answer is out there somewhere," Jake protested.

"Who is at Winchester?" Max asked.

"Well, there's Alfred somewhere, but his burial spot has never been found. Also, there are the six mortuary caskets in the cathedral and others buried at Hyde Abbey. They are all long-gone kings of Wessex and other locations."

Before they headed back to Broadway, Jake used all of his array of lenses and took a score of photos of the standing angel and its faint inscription. They would need further examination.

Back at the Lygon Arms Hotel, they assembled for dinner and thoughts of stalkers were temporarily forgotten. The excitement of their find had raised their spirits and given them hope for a successful outcome. They paid no attention to the usual woman sitting some distance away from them, engrossed in a book. If they had looked closer, they would have seen that the book had an oblong shape cut into it, in which rested her powerful listening device.

Bella spoke first. "If we go to Winchester cathedral, there's no way, whoever we are, that we would be given permission to open any of the six caskets. They have been as they are over the centuries and are regarded as sacrosanct. There have, I see, been many theories put forward as to whom is interred in them, and that includes Alfred the Great, who was later moved to Hyde Abbey, but his remains have never been found. But I still think we should look at the caskets. What do you all think?"

There was all-around agreement.

Kristy added more of what she knew. "I can tell you this, though, Bristol University has unlocked the caskets and has been studying what remains for some years now using carbon-fourteen techniques. Over 1300 bones have been recovered and twenty-three partial skeletons reconstructed.

THE MAGDALENE MISSION

The six mortuary chests are painted wooden caskets which were displayed high on stone screen walls on either side of the high altar area. These mortuary chests are the last in a series of similar arrangements for the safekeeping of the remains of many important kings and bishops who were originally buried in the Anglo-Saxon cathedral known as Old Minster, north of the present cathedral. The mortuary chests are believed to contain the pre-Norman Conquest remains of kings and bishops, but it had long been known that the bones were jumbled, rather than individual skeletons. Part of this confusion goes back to 1158, when the first group of royal and episcopal remains, reburied for a time after the demolition of Old Minster in 1093-4, were put into lead caskets near the high altar. An investigative researcher noted that 'kings were mixed with bishops.'

"A second group of royal bones, which had been reburied with greater care in the choir of the Norman cathedral, were later put into individual chests, but they seem to have been particular targets for the Roundhead soldiers who ransacked the cathedral in 1642 at the start of the English Civil War, so further mixing of the bones took place. Although the chests bear inscriptions stating who was supposed to be within them, it was clear they bore no relation to the actual contents – and the names of other individuals also said to be in the chests are known only from antiquarian writings. I don't think we are going to see anything new there, but we may glean some important information. Clearly, Jacques de Molay's casket was not among them. Research continues to this day and may go on for more years yet."

Bella added a further comment. "After that, we should go to nearby Hyde, where Edward the Elder is buried and, if not successful, we can go to Brookwood, in Surrey, to look at

Edward the Martyr, who – at the moment – is my favourite."

"Why is that?" Max asked.

"Simply because Marion was no ordinary peasant. She was of noble lineage and her family, I found out, had French connections. She wed a French knight and stands in direct line to the first Earl of Surrey, William de Warenne, and his family. So, I've made a wild guess, with that as part of her make-up and tradition, she might well have favoured a king interred in Surrey, close to her heart. What do you think?"

"Another fanciful guess, but it's a possibility," Max added, "and I do agree we must leave no stone unturned. Okay, let's do Winchester first and see what that brings."

Across the room, the scholarly woman stood and with her flat, clumpy shoes, made a less-than-graceful exit from the room. She had heard all she needed.

At full volume, she played back the recorder for Croxley and Bull to listen to. They did so in silence.

Croxley spoke once it had finished. "Where is this Winchester place?"

"They said down south a couple of hours, and they might be stopping overnight. We can easily track them. They seemed excited and on to something."

"Well, give me the recorder. I'm going to Skype our bishop and play it back to him and see what his reaction might be. The last thing we want is for him to cancel the operation. We need his bonus money and if that team finds what they are looking for, we grab it and it certainly will not be for Bishop Ignatius, unless he makes a higher bid than anybody

THE MAGDALENE MISSION

else's. All agreed?"

Such was Croxley's hold over them that there was no disagreement.

Chapter 27

Winchester City

The journey was uneventful. Throughout, they kept constant watch behind them, but there was nothing to report. Once parked, they made their way to the cathedral, but stopped to admire the imposing statue of King Alfred that overlooked the main street.

It was not long after that the cathedral's magnificent and imposing structure came into view.

Jake set to with his camera. "This building never fails to impress me, and I've seen it so many times."

The agreement was mutual.

Once inside, they gazed appreciatively at the ornate structures all around them. Traces still remained of colourful early frescos before most were abolished after King Henry's declaration of an English Church, free from Rome.

Slowly, they approached the altar, as if in a state of reverence at what was being displayed. The six caskets were in a row.

"Amazing." Max wasn't normally taken aback. "But if they have all been examined and continue to be so, and no trace of

THE MAGDALENE MISSION

Alfred the Great or de Molay's gold casket or a Magdalene Gospel has been found, then clearly, as I see it, we are very much in the wrong location."

"Not necessarily so," Bella replied. "It helps validate our research and what our dissertation will be when we present it."

King Alfred

"Well, let's get as close as we need and can. They are inspiring, that I cannot deny."

They moved around and decided to buy all the photographs they could, as taking their own was not allowed. They failed to notice a burly black leather jacketed man and an overly made-up, flashily dressed woman with their arms linked not far behind them and watching their every move.

Later, Isabella's team walked out into the bright sunshine and headed for a nearby pub, the Wykeham Arms, to discuss their next move. Once inside, they looked around but saw nothing and nobody suspicious.

"All clear." Max did a double take and found them a window table. They ordered drinks, and he remained on high alert.

Jake sat himself in a position where he could view the bar and the door to see who was coming in. He still saw nothing suspicious.

The place was full, and it was noisy, so any attempts to talk were done at a high volume.

Kristy spoke. "Two kings, Alfred the Great and Edward the Elder, are supposed to have been buried here, but no grave, casket, or any trace of anything to do with them has ever been found."

"Well, if we find nothing here, we will be heading to Brookwood tomorrow. This is getting tiring, and I just hope our efforts have not been a waste of time." Max sounded weary. "And on top of that, we have been targeted by a nasty bunch of lunatics – religious, I don't doubt. It makes me wonder, with hindsight, what are we all doing here?"

"You know full well, Max, what you accepted, as we all do. No person could have foreseen what we have had to go through. Maybe if we had, we wouldn't have accepted the mission."

Not a word was spoken, and another round of drinks was gladly accepted.

An hour later, they paid the bill and made their way to Hyde Abbey, close by.

It was an uninspiring construction after the splendour of Winchester, and it was hard to believe that mighty kings might have been buried there. There were many references to Alfred, but no evidence of him anywhere, or anything that could link Jacques de Molay or Mary Magdalene.

They looked at every plaque and visible reference.

Max, again, with his linguistic abilities, found something that jolted him. On a small wall plaque, almost indecipherable, was a tiny inscription in Latin below an equally small crown. A king's crown accompanied by a small relief carving of what looked like a Templar emblem – a small cross – but it could have predated that.

"*'Nomina regni brevia erunt. Perfida caede capietur. Iesus, Maria Mater, Maria uxor Si inveneris eam sufficient.'*" Max read it aloud to the others. "In English, it says:

A namesake's reign will be but short.
A treacherous murder will him but halt.
Jesus, Mary Mother, Miriam wife
If you find her it will suffice.

"Holy shit, Nostradamus is alive and well! Who the hell wrote that?" shouted Jake, with uncharacteristic language. "And when?"

"Wow!" Bella shouted too. "The namesake has to be Edward the Martyr. His reign was short, and he was murdered, and now his remains are at Brookwood. This has to be what we've been looking for. That verse says it all, doesn't it?"

Max spoke. "It does, and I think we're on to something big here."

"Yes," added Kristy. "It looks as if we alone have been led along a mysterious path that nobody on earth has ever trod before. What do you think?"

"I'm not into this mystical crap," Max added, "but something is very odd about what has been happening to us. Do we all agree?"

No disagreement.

"This is weird." Bella looked perplexed. "I think we have found what we need. To here. Tomorrow, we head out to Brookwood in Surrey."

There was no dissent.

Isabella felt a shift in her perceptions and in her mind. Doors were tentatively opening, and she had no idea where they may lead.

Something was occurring within her, and she could not explain it to herself or others.

Alexa played with the handle of her titanium-bladed scalpel, looking forward to being able to use it once again. Secretly, in the depths of her mind, she had an idea or two. She had one person in particular in mind whom she might use to further Croxley's ambitions. A picture of her intended actions flashed through her mind, and now she had to confirm with him that this was an award-winning strategy. Firstly, she would have to wait for them to find what they were looking for and, by the way they were behaving and talking, she guessed that they were on to something.

THE MAGDALENE MISSION

The following day
St Edward the Martyr Orthodox Brotherhood
Brookwood

Situated in one of the world's largest cemeteries, the church looked captivating.

Kristy had, yet again, a goldmine of information about Edward and the status of the church. "Edward's reign was very short, and he was a deeply religious and devout soul. After his murder, he was hurriedly buried at Corfe Castle in Dorset. Not long after, strange lights were seen emanating from his grave and a host of miraculous cures began to occur to various people who had visited his grave. His remains were moved to Shaftesbury Abbey and eventually he was canonised. Then came the Dissolution of the Monasteries, and the monks hid his remains. To cut a long story short, his casket was discovered in modern times and, after lengthy negotiations, the Russian Orthodox Church – as it was then, before becoming part of the Greek Orthodox Church – accepted all the conditions asked for canonisation. He was accepted as a saint and a shrine was erected. Now, mark this. Long before the shrine and the iconostasis were in place, all those centuries ago, at his initial interment, amongst the attendees were the first Earl of Surrey, William de Warenne, and his French family. Marion, as we now know, was in his lineage. Now, what do you think? This has to be our most promising lead yet."

They headed slowly to the abbey's church.

"Look at that!" exclaimed Bella. "That's beautiful. It has a style and a flavour of its own. The monks here run the church, as it is also a monastic community. The Orthodox tradition knew how to present things. Let's get inside and look at his shrine."

They all felt overwhelmed. The entire place throbbed with unseen life. It had a living atmosphere about it.

"Look," Jake said, "the shrine is over there."

They headed towards it.

All four gasped, and then there was not a sound to be heard.

"It is stunning." Bella appeared moved.

Max replied, "It certainly has something going for it. Religions can be beautiful, but the trouble is they are often ruined by ugly people."

They ignored him.

"Let's get closer." Kristy edged forward.

All around the walls were mounted icons and flickering candles. The team felt like intruders and their unwashed feet treading on the wooden floors did not seem right. Nearby, a monk moved over to talk to them. He was friendly and had a warm smile.

Years of meditation and prayer shone from him like the evening star. His habit and cowl were of black wool. The pitch of his voice was soft and gentle.

"Hello, friends, and welcome. I am Brother Macarius. I am in charge of this shrine to Saint Edward, and the iconostasis. May I help you in any way?"

Isabella returned his greeting and quietly began her lengthy explanation of their mission and how they had arrived at his church. She made no mention of the scary events that followed them from place to place.

"I think we should all sit down. Your backing and

credentials are truly impressive. We find this intriguing. I would like to hear more and see if we can help you and at the same time, maybe help ourselves. There are many of us in our brotherhood who would be in favour of your mission – and of course, there are others who would not. The Magdalene, I feel, was sent by God to accompany his blessed child, Jesus. As you suggest, was he married to her? She is often referred to as his 'companion.' In Jewish terms, that would mean she was his wife and partner. Translations are often in error. I have read through the Gospel of Mary Magdalene, and it is indeed intriguing, and as you have said, there are clearly omissions. If all of this is true, it is not a threat, but can only strengthen my belief in this extraordinary episode and the divine nature of Christ. Your story of Jacques de Molay and his heart, I have not heard before. If the lady you name Marion placed the missing texts in a gold casket, I've never heard of that too. Yes, Saint Edward's remains are here and his casket has never been opened." Brother Macarius paused, looking reflective.

A bell tolled.

"I must go now. My daily Offices of Supplication are now needed. Visit me again tomorrow, as today, and I will tell you what we can do for you."

Chapter 28

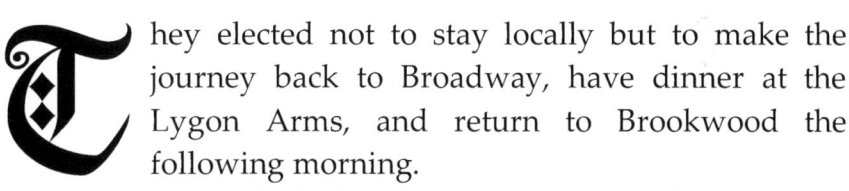

They elected not to stay locally but to make the journey back to Broadway, have dinner at the Lygon Arms, and return to Brookwood the following morning.

At dinner, Isabella led the conversation. "That was one productive visit and, with any luck, may prove positive. If it wasn't for your historical knowledge, Kristy, we wouldn't have made it to that church."

"Save it," Kristy replied. "We still have to gain access to the casket and, come what may, if we find anything, it will belong to the Orthodox Church, right?"

Max spoke. "You're right, Kristy. Should anything be found, a lot of investigation and negotiations are going to be needed to reach some sort of understanding or settlement. But, hey, we haven't found anything yet, but this is the closest anybody has ever been."

"One thing we seem to have omitted," Jake added. "Haven't we forgotten our stalkers? They have been quiet of late. Shouldn't we now be on maximum alert? What we are seeking they seem to want too, and they are never far away—"

THE MAGDALENE MISSION

Bella interrupted, "Look, we could be on the verge of a major breakthrough here and we are not going to be deterred. Whoever they are, what more can they do?"

"Well, they've fired guns and nearly hit us, and we could have been killed. That's something we should not dismiss. Sure, they have been quiet for a bit and if they know that we are on the verge of an amazing discovery our lives may become more dangerous." Kristy looked pale.

Across the room sat the academic-looking woman engrossed in her thick Russian literary book with a banner heading, Eugene Onegin by Alexander Pushkin. It wasn't that. It was a hollowed-out version containing a concealed listening device. It worked well. She didn't miss a word.

Thirty minutes later, she reported back to Croxley.

He looked grim. "I've been talking with the bishop, and I played the previous recording for him. He is still far from happy and is almost demanding action. I tried explaining to him that our team of treasure hunters seems to be excited about something, but he is insisting on a positive result soon or our task will come to a swift end."

"Don't despair, Matthew." Alexa was eager to tell him what she had heard. "Just listen to this. They think they are on to something. Let me play it back to you." Without waiting for an answer, she switched the player on.

They listened in silence.

Croxley spoke. "Well, that throws a whole new perspective on things. It looks promising. God is leading us, indeed. So, they are meeting people tomorrow. I want to see this place and what actually may happen."

"I thought you might. My tracker and bug are securely in place, so tomorrow it is. Let's hope we get something we can tell Ignatius."

"Oh, I'm sure we will. They are all excited like never before since this started. So, tomorrow it is this Brookwood place."

That morning, the sun shone brightly as the research team made an early start with hopes held high. They were, however, on high alert but there was not a person or vehicle that appeared to be tracking them. They didn't drop their guard, and their state of high alert continued. The journey would be one hundred miles, a couple of hours driving.

The trip gave them no cause for alarm and had been uneventful. The massive cemetery had a quietness that indicated that there was nobody around. The St Edward the Martyr Orthodox Church soon came into view. It appeared peaceful and tranquil.

The doors were locked so Jake knocked on them loudly. Within minutes, they slowly opened, and Brother Macarius stood in front of them. His smile, as before, was wide and welcoming. With him stood a severe-looking older monk. He was introduced as the igumen – or, as one would normally say, the abbot – Abbot Gregory.

His stern countenance was misleading. A broad smile made a transformation and Bella thought years had fallen from him.

He spoke with a voice that rang like a booming church

bell, loud and clear. "Friends, my learned brother Macarius has briefed me on the nature of your quest. Intriguing, indeed. Will you follow me to my private chamber, where I would like to learn as much as you can tell me, in detail." He signalled them to follow him down a small corridor with wall-mounted crucifixes every yard or so on both sides before ascending a small flight of stone steps.

Soon they were in a room that was plain and simple yet adorned with numerous religious icons and crucifixes bearing agonised images of Christ.

They were offered tea and biscuits and Bella was determined not to miss a thing. She began at the very beginning with their visit to the Berlin Museum, then on to Israel, India, and Portugal. She did not miss a detail, or the possible interpretations and consequences if any of this could be proved. The only issue she avoided was the menace their stalkers had given them. She also went into detail about her major sponsors and why they sought to find the alleged transcripts.

The abbot listened to everything she had to tell him. When she had finished, he gave her a slight smile before sipping his tea. "Thank you for that, Professor Vanton. Most intriguing. You do seem to be guided by the will of God. There are those here who would deeply disapprove of your venture and talk of the Magdalene, and of Issa, especially of him possibly being a Buddhist monk. I must say, being married to her would be considered the pinnacle of outrageous heresy. Any such investigation they would attempt to block and ban for eternity. True or untrue as your quest may be, we should not be afraid of it. The story of Jacques de Molay, his heart, and the Gospel of the Magdalene are the stuff of heretical novels. I am fascinated by it. If it is untrue, we have nothing to fear. If proven true, we may have everything to gain.

"Since Emperor Constantine's era, misogyny has prevailed in our Christian church. I am opposed to that. What I am about to propose is in deepest secrecy between us all here, including Brother Macarius, who I know shares my more liberal views. Any knowledge of an investigation and opening of the casket would provoke outrage here. Therefore, it must be done in total secrecy. The only way that can be achieved is during the latest and earliest of hours, when all my monks will be asleep. Two nights from now, at eleven o'clock, I will retire with Brother Macarius to the iconostasis and shrine room for deep, undisturbed meditation and prayer. You will join us but leave your vehicle some distance from here. At that time, you will be given entry. Once inside, we will proceed to the tomb and set about opening it. Please bring whatever tools you think will be required and we should soon discover how correct your previous discoveries have been. We are familiar with stories surrounding the Templars and of Jacques de Molay, but not the story you have revealed. So, until then, I will take my leave of you, and with my brother, we will see you in two nights' time." Placing his palms together as in prayer, Abbot Gregory gave a slight bow, turned, and with the monk, left the room.

The return journey was one rife with an air of excited anticipation. They were completely unaware that they had been trailed. Bella's team had, in their animation, all but forgotten their stalkers.

THE MAGDALENE MISSION

Croxley, Alexa, and Bull were never far behind, and the excited body language of their prey had not gone unnoticed.

The research team drove back to the Lygon Arms. They argued that after the attack on the house, it would be safer and wiser to spend as much time at the hotel as they could. There would be less chance of a repetition of the firearm attack.

Once in the dining area, they performed their now-customary scan check of diners. All seemed clear and beyond suspicion. Finding a vacant table, they sat and began to discuss the day's events.

"That was unbelievable." Max looked animated. "Those two guys are so not typical narrow-minded religious people. It was unreal, almost unbelievable, the way the abbot and the monk reacted to what you told them, Bella. They seemed to want to know as much as we do."

Jake replied, "That may be so, but if we find nothing, what then?"

"We can only cross that bridge when we get there. What we should be considering is the possibility that we do find what we are seeking. There would be problems for the abbot, and also for us. What would be done with such a discovery?"

"We would then have to bring in the sponsors for negotiations. It would not be for us to make any sort of deal – we have not been given that authority."

"Well, we have a free day tomorrow and most of the following day after," Max pointed out. "All we have to do is be at the church by eleven in the evening and the fun will begin. At least it will give us a chance to decide how we can go about such a find. I've been sending frequent reports to all our backers, so they have a good idea where we're at. I never mentioned any of the attacks we have suffered. I didn't want them pulling the rug from under our feet. Not when we've got this far."

"I'm still on edge." Kristy spoke. "It's all gone quiet, too quiet, like the calm before the storm. We mustn't drop our vigilance, not one bit. From the way they have always found us, there has to be a good chance they know our every move and exactly what we are planning."

"I second that." Jake stood up as he spoke and did another visual scan of the dining area. "Nobody and nothing suspicious I can see from here."

He totally ignored the stooped academic-looking woman sitting across the room. She was wearing a heavy, pleated tweed skirt, and a thick cardigan adorned with a row of old-fashioned pearls. Balanced on her nose were the pince-nez glasses she always wore, which seemed to compliment her greying hair, tied in an untidy bun. As usual, she appeared to be reading a heavy Russian novel. There was a noticeable smirk on her face.

Max looked thoughtful. "I don't trust anybody around here. There are only a few people but everyone is suspect, as far as I'm concerned, and that includes that studious old bat over there, engrossed in a book."

"Come to think of it, Max," said Jake, "yes, she has always been here when we are, and I don't recognise any of the other diners being here before. What do you think?"

"We have no evidence, and she looks harmless enough. Take a look around and get in close to see what you can."

"Okay." Jake pushed back his chair and with an air of disinterested casualness, began to walk closer to the seated woman.

There was a sharp snap as she abruptly closed her novel. She lifted her glass and took a large gulp before swinging her head around to stare directly over the tops of her glasses at the approaching Jake.

He felt awkward and uncomfortable and avoided her pointed stare. At the same time, he moved away from her, aware that her gaze was fixed upon him. Trying to act nonchalantly, he steered himself back to the others. He could see, when he reached them, that they looked concerned. He turned to look the way he came from, but there was no sign of the woman. She had gone.

"Damn! It has to be her. How did she know I was heading her way, making her close her book and stare intently at me?"

"Good question," Bella said. "It was noticeable. As soon as you got close, she seemed to know, and now she has vanished. We saw it all."

"Unless she had a listening device, there would be no way she knew what you were up to. We have no proof, but from now on, any single woman nearby has to be a suspect. I would put money on it – she is a stalker." Max looked at them all and there was unanimous agreement.

They stayed as long as they could before heading back to Kristy's home and gratefully going to bed. The damage from the shooting had been repaired and the place looked as it had before.

They planned, for the following two days, to start collating all their evidence, ready to begin assembling it in a presentable form.

Croxley listened to what Alexa had to say and to her recording. "You are right. They suspect single women and no matter what you try, you would be a target for their attention.

Hopefully, that will end soon. It's clear they intend to go to that church late at night. We will be there also, and ready to strike. Between us, we have two guns and some nasty blades. With these, if they are successful, we will take what they find and get away fast. We will hold all the aces and there will be nothing they can do about it. Also, it will be a pleasure informing our fat bishop what we have. I've been considering this carefully. I am certain the Catholics will up their offer for those writings, if ever they're found. We will want funds placed in our untraceable account. When they are, we of God's Chosen Evangelist Church will never let him have what he is paying for. It will be our sacred weapon, to strike fear into all false believers."

Alexa looked across to Bull and gave him a thin-lipped smile. They had already discussed their possible plan of action should the text be found.

He gave her a small, discreet nod.

Croxley didn't notice.

Chapter 29

The hours passed slowly. Much writing and analysis had taken place and their composition was beginning to take shape. Skilfully blended in were the countless photographs from every place they had visited. Pictures of de Havilland's sword and shield, together with the story of de Molay's heart, were not omitted, and also references to de Havilland's marriage to Marion and her ancestral link to the family of William de Warenne, Earl of Surrey. All were able to trace a lineage back to King Edward the Martyr, and ultimately to Alfred the Great. King Edward had been canonised and declared a saint, and his remains were now interred in the church they had twice visited.

Their expectations were high that the greatest was yet to come.

The afternoon before they were to leave, they had seen nothing to suggest that they were being watched or followed

KEN FRY

in any way. Max and Jake set about assembling some tools. They picked out crowbars, spades, and axes, together with handfuls of metal strips that they thought might be useful. The ladies assembled photographic equipment of all sorts, sheets, sacking, and anything else they could find to use as protection for anything they potentially discovered.

Darkness had descended and they made the decision to proceed to the church, a good two-hour night-drive away. They checked in every direction as best they could, but there were no signs of any stalkers. It was all clear. With hopes riding high, they went out together, each checking a separate direction before getting into the car and setting off.

With constant checking all around them, there was no indication that they were being followed.

Not far away, their departure was noted, and another vehicle began the long journey behind them, but out of visual range. The three occupants were all armed.

"We've had nobody behind us apart from what you might expect from local traffic." Max sounded optimistic.

"I'll believe that once we get there and return safely." Isabella was not that optimistic. "Don't forget, whoever they are, they have always managed to be wherever we go, so be prepared and expect the unexpected."

"Bella's right," Kristy joined in. "Not until this mission is over and we are safely home will I feel safer, and not even then, after that shooting. How the hell did they know where we were?"

"We have no idea," added Jake, "but these people seem

THE MAGDALENE MISSION

professional, and whatever we have done, they are right behind us all the way."

"Look, guys, quiet for a moment. We are almost there. I'm going to switch off all our lights and park outside the car park, as requested. Jake and I will carry the tools, and Bella and Kristy, please bring the photographic gear and whatever else you loaded. When that's done, we keep together and make our way over. Okay?"

They all nodded.

It was dark and totally silent, apart from trees rustling in a slight breeze. They quickly unloaded their equipment and made their way across to the church.

"Look," said Bella, "there's a flickering light coming from the shrine area. It has to be candles. It must be the abbot and Brother Macarius. We are on time, as agreed, so let's knock and see what happens. "

Three sharp loud raps on the door were quickly answered by Brother Macarius, who spoke in hushed tones. "Welcome, friends." He held his finger to his lips to indicate the need for quiet. "Abbot Gregory is ready and waiting."

They loaded their equipment in and wondered how they could be quiet with the tools they had assembled.

Abbot Gregory beckoned them over through the iconostasis, which was reverently aglow with flickering shadows caused by the soft flutter of candlelight. The air was smoky and full of the subtle aroma of billowing frankincense that penetrated every corner, nook, and cranny.

Soon, they entered Saint Edward's shrine room.

The abbot spoke. "You are not required to do what you see us do, but just respectfully observe."

Both the abbot and Brother Macarius fell to their knees, making several signs of the cross as they did so. There followed three full-length prostrations by both religious men.

The team, not knowing the protocol, retreated slightly and simply bowed their heads.

The muffled sound of a nearby slow-moving vehicle outside went unnoticed.

The holy duo arose from their observances.

"There's no need for you to feel awkward. We would be feeling the same in your world," the abbot told them. "This is his casket." He walked to the prominent golden structure beneath a curved four-post archway illuminated with soft lamps and candles. Numerous icons, pictures of saints, and crucifixes overlooked the entire area. He waved them closer. "It has not been opened since the early Medieval Age."

Isabella looked concerned. "Dear God, I really do not think we should be doing this. It's a form of pillage. I feel uneasy."

The team looked apprehensive.

"There's no reason you should." The abbot spoke kindly. "It is my decision, and I could have refused you, but I have not. I am deeply curious, and the decision is entirely mine, so have no fears or remorse. Saint Edward has been around for many years, and I am certain he knows by now how to look after himself – and us too, if need be. Now, enough said. Please continue. As qualified researchers and archaeologists, I am certain you will be most careful."

"Thank you, Abbot." Max spoke in a hushed whisper. It seemed appropriate. "Jake and I will do the manual work. Kristy and Isabella will first take photographs of the entire casket and all its fittings, one by one. Once that's done, we can try and open it. It may be easy or difficult. We will soon find out."

The silence of the room was broken only by the click of

each camera shot and the hushed voices of Brother Macarius and the abbot offering up prayers and chants.

The shots were taken, and close inspection of the tomb began.

Max bent close to look at the fastenings around the coffin. After a while he stood. "The fastenings are of metal and wood. The sarcophagus is made of wood and some stone. Fortunately, the lid structure is mostly wood. The entire top of the casket is one solid and very heavy plank covered in a layer of some sort of gold mixture. Most wood caskets use a simple metal clasp that technically does not lock the casket, but it does prevent anybody opening it without a hard struggle.

"Once we unhinge it, we may be able to slide the lid along, but that may be more difficult than we think and will require muscle power. Before we do, we have an endoscope and monitor screen, which will allow me to ascertain what is in there. All I need to do is slide it in under the corner and move it along, if I can, and we should get some sort of picture of what's in there. But first we must disconnect the hinges. This is how to do it." He placed a thin feeler gauge of rigid, solid steel under the clasp, and, with a certain amount of firm effort, there was a metallic click, and the first one was freed. There was no damage, and it could easily be reconnected. He handed Jake another gauge. "You start on the other side, Jake. We have six of these to do."

"Please be careful." Abbot Gregory looked concerned.

"Don't worry, Abbot. I've done this sort of thing many times in the past, and never failed yet."

Ten minutes later, the last clasp was unfastened and not one was damaged.

They all crowded expectantly around.

Max inserted the endoscope's wafer-thin end and it slid, without too much difficulty, under the corner. With great caution, he edged it along as best as possible. The screen began to flutter with a series of flashing lines before it began to steady and transformed into a stable and recognisable state, and an image began to form.

"Look, there's something there." Max jabbed the screen with his finger.

Six pairs of eyes were clued in as the unmistakeable image of what appeared to be some sort of shrouded body came into focus.

"Praise be to God!" The abbot was animated, along with Brother Macarius.

Bella held her breath. "Yes," she said, "there's definitely something there that looks as if it was once a body."

"Well, if there wasn't, we would all be wasting our time here and the church would have a problem," Kristy remarked. "We want to see the possibility of another smaller gold casket, hopefully containing what we have come to look for – a papyrus or something similar, together with what once was a heart."

"Look! Look!" Bella all but yelled. She pointed excitedly at the screen.

Sure enough, there was the unmistakeable outline of something that clearly wasn't a body. It looked like a rectangular shape, small in size, unclear on the screen, but needing their immediate attention.

Both monks, with heads bent, began a series of Latin prayers.

Inch by inch, Max guided the instrument around the gilded coffin and spent more time looking at the shrouded form. Their excitement was palpable.

THE MAGDALENE MISSION

Once he had examined the entire casket, he stood straight. "Well, you've all seen what there is to be seen. I think it's time to attempt to remove this coffin top. Over here, Jake, we need to start heaving. If we are lucky, it should begin to slide."

"Let me help too." Brother Macarius joined them.

"Thanks, Brother. You and Jake take the sides and I'll take the centre. On the count of three we begin to heave. One… two… three… heave!"

All three grunted loudly, tugging hard at the top. Brother Macarius's cowl fell back, exposing the whiteness of his shaven head.

There was slight movement and the sound of wood scraping on something, but it *did* move.

"Again," Max demanded, and the process was repeated over and over until half the contents were revealed to the world.

The abbot spoke. "This is amazing, but what do we do now?"

"What we do, Abbot," spoke Isabella, "is first, when we can reach the small casket properly, we pull it out and see if we can open it. If we can, and if what we find inside is what we are hoping to find, it will prove Marion, wife of de Havilland the Templar, has placed this here. It may be the remains of Jacques de Molay's heart. It should also – more importantly for all of us here – contain the missing text of the Magdalene's gospel. That should be conclusive evidence that this is truly the resting place of Saint Edward the Martyr."

"Come on, then, three more tugs should give us access," Max cajoled them.

This time, it moved more easily and soon all that they wished for came into full view. Cleary, there were the remains of what had once been a human being, wrapped in a thick winding shroud. It was surprisingly dust free. Behind it was the shimmering, elongated gold casket.

They stood back and looked at it. Not a word was spoken, nor a hand extended to touch it. The silence seemed like an eternity.

The abbot took the initiative. With tremulous care, he crossed himself and then sprinkled holy water onto the casket, leant forward, clasped it with firm hands and, inch by inch, dragged it clear of the shroud until he managed to hold it up and place it on a flat surface.

Macarius went to his knees and bowed his head.

The team moved away. This was clearly an emotional moment for the monks.

The casket was plain, apart from a small crucifix affixed to the top.

The abbot asked Max, "Can you open this? I don't have the skills."

Max, aware of the sensitivity of what he was about to attempt, gave a rare gesture of care and humility. He gently picked up the casket and bowed his head slowly and held it that way for several seconds. Using his loupe, he scoured every part of it.

He looked up and nodded. "This will be easy. The top is not fastened, but just a tight fit and sealed with bitumen and wax, which will come away easily. You see, it has a slightly protruding bitumen edge all the way around, which acts as an airtight seal. It has been that way since it was made and placed here. Abbot, I propose that I will gently strip away the seal with my folding Spyderco pocket-knife, which I've used countless times in the past. It never fails. The bitumen is easily replaced by heating it, and nobody would know it had been cut away. Are you happy for me to proceed?"

THE MAGDALENE MISSION

Abbot Gregory did not hesitate. "Please, Doctor Franklin. I trust you all, so kindly proceed." He waved his hand across to the casket.

Max produced his knife and with only the slightest hesitation he carefully began stripping away the seal, keeping it as a continuous strip to reseal it when needed. Soon it was completed and totally removed.

Everyone was silent.

"The moment of truth, everybody." Max looked up at five anxious faces and began inching the lid away.

What happened next caused them all to gasp. From the small opening, released after centuries, arose a green vapour coupled with a beautiful scent, like that of a thousand roses.

Isabella covered her mouth with her hands. "Oh, dear God, what is that?"

The vapour permeated the entire shrine room. Everybody looked shocked. The monks fell to their knees.

Max stayed calm. He had no option but to proceed. He pushed the lid back farther until it was completely clear, and the contents were once more exposed to the world.

Six transfixed people stared down in a state of amazement.

There appeared to be two items. The smaller was wrapped in a thick purple velvet material. The other was rolled and resembled papyrus or very ancient leather. It was bound with several swirls of colourful twine. The colour was fresh and alive. Not one piece of the two items looked the worse for wear. They looked as if they could have been placed there yesterday.

"This is nothing short of miraculous," Max remarked. "I've never seen anything like it in all the years I've done this sort of work."

KEN FRY

The scent persisted and did not diminish.

Pulling on surgical gloves, the team decided to examine the two items. The first thing was to unwrap the purple cloth to see what was there.

With great care, Max – with his skill and expertise in archaeological matters and using fine tweezers – began to unwrap the smaller item. It had been carefully covered and it wasn't until he pulled the last fold of cloth back that the item was revealed.

It was a heart. An almost-living heart that looked as if it had just been removed and had only just stopped beating. It looked fresh and alive.

Kristy held on to Bella and began to weep. "It just can't be! It can't be!"

Jake said nothing and concentrated on getting as many shots as he could.

Bella turned to the abbot and with a shaky voice said, "No doubt, Abbot, that the one who is under that shroud is your beloved saint."

"By all the saints in heaven, this is a miracle ordained by God and Christ himself! I swear to God, I thought I saw that heart beat for a few moments. Please return it to its resting place, I beg you."

"I would add the Magdalene's name to that statement, Abbot, and yes, it will be done, but first I need to see what the other object is. I think we all know. It has to be what we have been searching for across the world. Let's check it right now. No." She pushed down her excitement. "We should be doing this in laboratory-controlled conditions, not here in a chapel." She turned. "Abbot, with our written pledges to return, or whatever you wish, would you be willing for us to take this wrapped scroll for clinical examination? I think we should leave de Molay's Templar heart where it has been resting for centuries. It will, however, play a major part in our final report."

The abbot turned to Isabella. "Of course, but I must insist that we open it right now, and once we know what we are looking at, you have my permission. The heart must never leave its resting place and will stay here until the end of time. Once you have confirmed the authenticity of the manuscript, we will, on its return, decide on what we must do with it."

"Of course, Abbot. That goes without saying. We have a duty to our backers and their academic concerns. We will need to speak to them. Would you be prepared to do the same?"

"Yes, of course. Now, please unwrap the parchment. I am more than a little curious."

The team kept their surgical gloves on as, slowly and with the greatest of care Max, again using the tweezers, began to unravel the twine that bound the rolled parchment. Again, it looked as if it had been wrapped the same day. There were no signs of age or deterioration. It fell silently away from that which it had protected for so long.

Willingly and with full acceptance.

More scent, tantalising … beguiling

The only audible sound was the faint whirr of Jake's video camera.

When the binding had fallen away, Max looked around at them. "Well, this is it. We may even find out where that scent is coming from."

With a cautious nudge, he began to slowly unroll the ancient item. It offered no resistance. It seemed to be willing Max to continue. Soon it was unfurled to its full extent. Again, using his loupe, Max bent low and carefully scoured each letter. The item was a dusty brown and was made of papyrus. Of that he was certain. The small black lettering again looked as if it was recent, but he knew it could not be. "It seems to be written in Aramaic ... C-14 testing would be able to reveal more information."

Speaking directly to the abbot, he said, "It looks as if we have the *original* missing ten pages here – that's, the first six and the last four. It's like finding a pharaoh's tomb. This is astonishing! This has to be genuine."

Everyone stood staring at it.

"What does it say?" the abbot asked.

"I can't tell you until I've checked it all out, but you will be the first to know, Abbot. Hell, I can't stop looking at it in sheer amazement. Let me roll it back up. Jake, have you taken all the photos we will need?"

"Just a few more and I'll be done." Soon he looked up. "I'm finished here."

"Good. We will replace the heart exactly as we found it and close the casket. I'll use the cloth and cardboard rolls we brought along for the manuscript. It looks as if it will fit perfectly."

It did.

When he was done, he held it up for all to see and at that precise moment, they heard a loud crash outside, followed by a blast of cold air. As they swung around, they saw the side door had been kicked open and standing in the doorway were three figures dressed from head to toe in black and wearing balaclavas. Two were carrying suppressed pistols and the other a vicious-looking blade.

Chapter 30

Bishop Ignatius pushed away his empty dinner plate and took a copious swallow of his favourite finest Kopke port from a silver goblet. With the back of his hand, he wiped clean his fat, greasy lips. A warm glow of satisfaction coursed through him. An excellent meal plus the news he had received earlier had elevated his satisfaction. That information looked far more encouraging than previous bulletins.

The Magdalene scenario appeared to have taken a promising step forward. Matthew Croxley's news that morning was indeed favourable. His targets were being closely monitored and it was apparent they were on to something. What he found hard to believe was that the search was ending, or so it appeared, in *England* of all places, and not the Holy Land. He would have put money on the latter, if anybody had wanted to place a bet. It seemed the missing pages could be in the shrine room of a Georgian Orthodox church.

Now, that's amazing. If true, how did it get there? I must go to this place and not let Croxley's clumsy hands spoil it before I get a chance to look at it and confirm whether is genuine or not.

Next, he called his secretary and booked a flight to Gatwick. He would avoid London's Westminster Catholic Cathedral, as they were too pope-friendly, and his scheme could be discovered. Instead, he would stay at the important Roman Catholic Church of Saint Teresa of Avila at nearby Chiddingfold in Surrey where he had personal friends and important contacts.

He waited for over an hour and received no reply.

Something is wrong. Why hasn't Croxley replied? I need to speak to him.

He sat back down and sent another email to Croxley. After another hour's wait, he received a reply.

"Bishop, we are in the middle of pulling off something big here. Cannot talk. Go to Chiddingfold. We don't have time to arrange anything for you or collect you. Will get back to you when we have more news."

Ignatius felt affronted. *I don't like the sound of this. His news had better be good, or it could be the end of the line for him.*

Our fat friend is at a disadvantage. Croxley pondered. *Bishop Ignatius no longer holds all the aces. We stand on the edge of playing a winning hand. If tonight goes well, by God's grace, we will triumph in every possible way!*

He slapped his desk hard. It was going to be an interesting evening.

Several hours later, they had trailed the professor and her crew unnoticed – plus Croxley had the advantage of Alexa's tracking and listening device. They drove stealthily up to the church car park before turning the vehicle around as a precaution for a rapid exit. Bent double and as furtively as they could, they inched themselves up to the unlocked door. When they pressed their ears to it, such were the church's acoustics that they could hear every word that was spoken within. Croxley was beginning to believe with no uncertainty that here, indeed, was the missing manuscript. Every word he heard confirmed that belief. Sensing that they were about to leave, he knew it was time to strike. He signalled the other two.

With an almighty kick, Bull booted the door, which burst open like a puppet on a string.

Brandishing their weapons, they rushed in. They were met with astonishment and fear.

"Hold it right there!" Croxley confidently shouted beneath his all-concealing balaclava.

Alexa and Bull moved forward, threateningly brandishing their hardware.

Isabella and her companions had no doubt who they were, but were rendered speechless, with jaws agape.

"What is the meaning of this?" the abbot shouted, moving forward. "How dare you!"

Croxley gave him a shove backwards. "Sit down, old man, spawn of Satan, or you will get something you won't possibly like."

"Enough!" shouted Brother Macarius, striding forward.

Bull stepped towards him and smashed the butt of his gun into the monk's face, followed by a rock-hard fist. Just the moment he had been waiting for.

The brother hit the floor like a weightlifter's barbell. Blood oozed from both his head and mouth.

The abbot rushed to him.

"No farther!" Bull shouted. "Or you will get the same." He moved across to intercept the abbot.

Kristy began to move to the injured monk but the sharp feel of a large titanium scalpel on her face halted her in her tracks.

"One more step, darling, and you won't have a face to look at in the morning."

Kristy felt the slightest of nicks as a trickle of blood began a journey down her cheek and across her mouth. She could taste it and froze.

Croxley's muffled voice addressed Max. "Hand it over, Doctor Franklin, or the girl gets ripped."

Bull, smiling, smashed his rock-hard fist into Bella's petrified face. "There's more to come, ladies, if he doesn't."

Croxley did not approve as he watched her reel backwards.

Max rushed over to her.

"Enough of that, right now, you two. That can come later, but not here." Croxley had not been expecting rough stuff but said nothing more. He moved towards Max and pointed his gun at him. "C'mon, Doc, be a good boy now and you won't be harmed. All you have to do is hand it over."

Max held the scroll tightly in his hands. "You know what this is?"

"If I didn't, why would I be chasing you across the planet? It's the missing pages from the so-called gospel of the whore Magdalene."

"I don't yet know if it is. I haven't read it through or translated any of it."

"And how long is that going to take?"

"About three days, if there are no problems." Max

sounded calm, although his brain was racing.

"Well, here are my demands. Start on it as soon as you can. We will contact you when your time is up. You will not talk to the police or any other agency. We are going to take your girlfriends for a little ride somewhere, you won't know where. Any fuckups from you and you can say farewell to your lovely ladies forever. Their departure from this earth at the hands of my two friends here will be long, slow, and painful."

"Don't harm them and I will do what you ask. Why do you want the papyrus? Who are you?"

"That's not your concern right now." He turned to the still-dazed brother and the abbot. "You two misguided, heretical fools will also observe my demands to the doctor. If you break them, the ladies will perish. That I promise you."

Abbot Gregory, pale and shaken, looked across at Dr Franklin.

Max nodded. "I know as much as you do, Abbot. I've no idea who these people are, but hardly a day has passed when we have not experienced some sort of trouble." He turned to the assailants. "I will do as you ask and so will these monks. If you harm even one hair on either of the ladies, then you will never see this manuscript again, but I will ensure the entire world will know of it."

He didn't know why he added the last part, but he had an underlying sense that would be the last thing they would want. He turned to the ladies. "I am so sorry, but this is the best I can do. Trust me, please. Your safety is way above an ancient text. I will not let you down. I promise you that with all my heart."

"Very touching and heartfelt, Doctor. Now, let's be gone." Croxley signalled to Bull and Alexa.

Alexa pulled on Kristy. "You know, I could slit your cheeks open from each corner of your mouth to your ears. That would be fun. Maybe that will happen later. So, get moving."

Croxley waved his pistol at Bella and Kristy as a gesture to get going.

Isabella gave Max a terrified look.

He was unable to do anything. Their safety was paramount.

Brother Macarius rose from his knees and made an attempted lunge at Croxley. He got nowhere.

Bull was quick. He tripped him up within two strides and stamped twice, hard, on his shaven head.

The monk groaned with pain before passing out.

The door slammed shut. For what seemed like an eternity, all was quiet.

Jake broke the silence. "Jesus, Max, what do we do now?"

"We help clean this place up and see to the abbot." He gestured at the seated monk. His head was down, and he looked beaten. Macarius, badly bruised and battered, was attempting to stand.

"Easy, Brother, easy." Jake hauled him up before seating him on a nearby chair.

Max addressed both monks. "I do not know who those three were, but you are owed an explanation." He then outlined the events and mishaps that had followed them from Berlin to the Middle East and Asia and back to Europe. "We have no idea who they are, but suspect they are from a fundamentalist faith of some sort who do not wish to hear or see evidence that might upset their cosy beliefs."

Jake spoke. "For the safety of our two women, Abbot, we must not involve the police, and certainly not at this stage.

None of us had any idea that this would happen, and we don't wish to damage or harm the reputation of your lovely church and shrine."

"You two kindly souls," Max added, "have been witness to a remarkable find, which could change the world as we know it when news of it becomes known. That, to an extent, relies on all of us. We do, however, have to inform our backers of what we have found and what is contained in this manuscript that Jake here has copiously videoed and photographed. Right now, our concern is for Isabella and Kristy. That's our priority at this time."

Abbot Gregory looked serious and there was sadness in his eyes. "Of course, of course. You must do what you have to. At this stage, I make no claims regarding what you have found, but only ask that you let me know what is contained in your findings. We will pray for you all, from this very moment. I think in Buddhist terms what is happening here is known as karma." He glanced at Brother Macarius, and both got to their knees, bowed their heads, and began to pray.

Max looked across to Jake, whose expression was as awkward as his own. They had no time to hang around.

"Abbot, we must hurry. We don't have a lot of time to spare. We have to leave right now but once I've read through it, I will let you know. We have our ladies' safety to consider above all else. We will be in touch as soon as we can."

Chapter 31

Isabella and Kristy had no idea where they were. Blindfolds plus gags performed their duties. The journey was almost silent. Their cell phones had been taken from them and their wrists bound. They were now completely in the hands of their abductors.

Isabella heard a phone ring and the man who had been called Matthew, the apparent leader, answered it. She heard him talking to the caller, whom he called Bishop Ignatius. She couldn't hear what the bishop was saying, but heard his location repeated by Matthew, her captor, as Chiddingfold and Saint Teresa of Avila. She made a mental note and if and when they got out of this mess it was an important clue. She also heard the man tell Ignatius they had rented a house and that was where they were being taken. Matthew told him their target had found what appeared to be the missing manuscript. Once translated, it would be handed over to him and his prisoners released. If it wasn't, then they would not see the light of another day. It was God's will.

She gulped. Whoever these people were, she only could think they were extreme Catholics, but her captors in no way

THE MAGDALENE MISSION

fit into that category – just the opposite.

From behind her blindfold, Bella sensed that day had broken. She felt calm and alert. This situation was not an everyday occurrence, but she had complete trust in Max and Jake, for they would do everything required to secure their safety.

It was sometime later that they felt their vehicle come to a halt and the engine was switched off. Bella assumed they had arrived. Mentally, she estimated they had been driving for about two hours and guessed they had travelled approximately a hundred miles, but in what direction there was no way of telling. Saying very little, their captors bundled them from the transport and into a large house adorned with copious wisteria and ivy. Their blindfolds were removed, together with the gags and restraints. The trio continued wearing their face coverings.

"Get comfortable, girls. This is to be your home for a few days. Hope and pray it's not your last." The speaker sounded female and American.

"Who are you? Why are you doing this? We have not harmed you in any way. Show yourself!" For her courage, Bella received a massive backhand swipe across her face, sending her reeling back into her chair.

"Shut your ungodly mouth, you vile, sinning whore. We ask the questions, not you. Pray you do not see our faces or by God's will, we will kill you, and not too quickly."

A surgical scalpel sliced inches from her eyes.

Bella wiped away a small trickle of blood flowing down her lip.

Kristy shook her head at Bella. "Leave it, Bella. We cannot win this."

Bella nodded and for a moment felt a tug of fear, not just

for herself, but for all of them. She was afraid, knowing Max as she did, that he would take risks. Their lives were far more important than a translation. It was clear their captors wanted not only a translation but also the entire manuscript. Who was the bishop that their leader had spoken to? What he had said made it clear that he was Catholic, but there was no way that these three could be. Who were they and why did they want the papyrus? She had no doubt at all it was what her team had set out to find. What would these screwballs want with it? One thing was clear – they were very dangerous and not afraid to use violence and possibly murder. She only hoped Max and Jake understood that much!

It was then that the door was unlocked, and the trio walked in. The woman held a tray on which a water jug and plastic cups had been placed. The biggest surprise was that they were now unmasked. The balaclavas had been removed.

Their leader, Matthew, spoke. "We had a discussion. Once all is clear to you, we will be long gone from here. You might be alive, or you might not. You do not know who we are and what we represent. Should you find out, it might be too late for you anyway. My companions can be very violent, as you have found out to your cost a few times. Your male friends, I am certain, know the danger you are in. They have a few days to come up with their findings. For your sakes, pray they are favourable."

Isabella stood and looked directly at him, unafraid. "We don't care who you are, but why do you want this so much? It could be helpful if we knew."

Croxley paused. "Sit back down, will you?" He then seated himself opposite her. Leaning forward, his hands formed a steeple, and a rare small, thin smile ventured across his mouth. "I don't mind letting you into why we want what

THE MAGDALENE MISSION

you have so assiduously looked for. What I won't tell you is who we are. We know you have influential sponsors or mentors who have been desperate to find what they think are the ten missing pages of the lying rubbish called the Gospel of Mary Magdalene, the bulk of which is located in the National Museum of Berlin. If what you have found proves to be that, then the media – most of which is owned by Jews, the killers of our Lord Jesus Christ – will have a field day that we will never hear the end of. Anything they can say to pour scorn on His teachings, they will not hesitate to use. Magdalene was a common prostitute, a whore, imagined by some as his wife and the mother of his children. Not long ago, such views would have invoked the death penalty on any who said or believed them. I'm all for the restoration of that. You are being led down a false trail to help undermine the true faith and belief in Jesus Christ as the son of Almighty God. Clearly, no smelly whore could have written what she allegedly did. If your man confirms it was by her, then clearly Judaism will have scored a major victory. You are being duped. If your findings suggest this, they must never reach the media. They must be destroyed. We will do that."

"You are of the Christian faith, then?" Bella ventured. "Are you Catholics? If not, what are you?"

"You ask too many questions. What and who we are is no concern of yours or your friends. What *should* concern you is that their mission is a successful and satisfactory one, from our point of view. All your lives may depend on it. My colleagues are not known for giving mercy or forgiveness."

He looked at his two followers. Bull Morello was twirling his gun this way and that with assured, dexterous skill. Alexa did no more than show her surgical knife and, with a slow gesture, imitated cutting someone's throat with it.

Kristy, trembling, grabbed Bella's arm and held it tightly. She was clearly afraid.

Bella was also, but she suppressed its presence, which then focussed on the pit of her stomach as unseen nervous twitches.

The tension was broken by the chirping sound of Croxley's cell phone. "Hello, Ignatius. What can I do for you?"

Isabella could make out the sound of somebody speaking but not what was being said. Her only clue was in Croxley's responses.

"No, not yet, but we have our prisoners, and the find is being worked on. Whatever the result, we will have it in our hands very shortly. Then you may see it."

There was more interchange with Croxley. "We are not far from you at Chiddingfold, and yes, meeting to view it will not be difficult. And yes, we all hope it is the right thing. Once you have it, I've no doubt it will be lost forever. The thing we all dread is that... if they confirm it as authentic, it will end up in some museum for the entire world to gawk at. That would be another nail in Christ's body."

Isabella was mentally putting together what clues she had gathered by listening to the sketchy conversations. She knew that the Catholic church in Chiddingfold was of major importance. Designed by a renowned architect and built in 1959, it was close to becoming a listed building. The name Ignatius was a powerful one in Catholic terms, with two renowned figures in its history. Both were saints, one early on at Antioch, and the medieval figure of Loyola. This Ignatius had been addressed as Bishop. The man had to be a Catholic.

But hadn't a recent pope declared Magdalene as a true follower of Christ and his favourite disciple? Clearly, there were many who disagreed with that proclamation, and they had an inbuilt misogynistic view of women's role in society as a whole. It looked as if this bishop was of that mould.

She said nothing. The puzzle was becoming clearer.

This bishop was a Roman Catholic die-hard, an anti-progressive reactionary, and somehow an alliance had been forged with both the highest and lowest in belief structures. Those three in front of her, from their remarks, represented some sort of raw, basic fundamentalist group, of which there were many in the USA. But which? She decided to keep her observations to herself.

A feeling of uneasiness rippled through the bishop's mind and body. Something Croxley had said had an ominous ring to it. They had obviously discovered something, but he had followed that up with the words, '*Then you may see it.*'

'May *see it*!' That seemed to indicate that Croxley was pulling a bait-and-switch. Surely not, with all the money he was being paid. Of course, it could have been a figure of speech. Whatever he'd meant, the feeling of unease persisted in him. He had always trusted his feelings and emotions and so far, they had always been right. They had guided him through his life.

What can I do? If they have truly found it, Croxley has a criminal record and I guess he could be capable of something underhanded. Maybe I made a bad choice. Yet he heads an evangelical mission and is a man of God. My colleagues approved of the choice. He was the perfect candidate, but those words of his have aroused my suspicions. I must remain alert and on guard at all times. I will have to wait and see.

Chapter 32

A concerned and worried-looking Max sat staring into space. He had no idea what to do next. Beside him was the rolled manuscript. Neither he nor Jake felt like examining their find. Their prime concern was the predicament of Bella and Kristy. Mutilation and death threats had been made against them and there was every reason to think that they were not made idly. These people, whoever they were, meant every word they'd said and had demonstrated that with their attacks on Bella and the team. Each of them had been targeted, one way or another, since Berlin.

"C'mon, Jake, let's get started. The sooner the job is done, the better chance we have of keeping our ladies safe."

"I've taken all the pictures I can," he responded. "What do you think?"

"I need to go through it piece by piece, page by page. It's in remarkable condition, far superior to the bulk of it in Berlin."

"Are you sure it's genuine?"

"More or less. The papyrus is definitely the same as that

in Berlin. What I can't understand is how pristine it appears."

"Well," said Jake, "there's a mystery here, and how about the heart? It looked as fresh as something from a butcher's display cabinet, and that beautiful aroma. It was astonishing."

"You are right. There's something here that seems beyond rational explanation. I am convinced this is the genuine script, but what is mind-boggling is that it's written in Aramaic and not Sahidic Coptic, like the Berlin Codex. That could possibly mean it was written by the Magdalene herself!" Max, in spite of their predicament, was still capable of academic amazement.

"That can never be proven, but it is the most tantalising thought. All that needs to be done is to translate it and I think we'll be in for a surprise. What our criminal friends will make of it, I can't imagine. I still do not understand why they want this so much. I must do this correctly, as two precious lives rely on it. Listen to this. It's taken me a couple of hours to get it right. The translation is from the first missing page. It is Magdalene who is speaking. I'm certain it was to the twelve disciples."

Yeshua is my light, my companion and is a flame to the entire world. You dwell in darkness, and it is through me you may find light. Trust his words, which I give to you as he has told me. Clarity will find you and disperse your darkness. You will become beacons to the men and women of this world. Open your minds to my words as given by our Parent to his Son and then to me. We have come to you from the lands of the East. My Master, Yeshua, was revered and has taught me much, which I give to you.

"Damn!" Jake let rip. "That's great, and you have only just started. I think I understand why they want this so much. It's dynamite. It will throw the entire Christian world into turmoil. They must want it destroyed… that's plain to see now."

"I agree," Max added. "Sadly, the photos you shot will not be accepted as primary evidence and can easily be disproved. They will not be seen as genuine evidence, although we both know with certainty that they are. Yet we have to hand everything over or lives may be lost. I couldn't have that on my conscience. We are caught in a deadly snare and unless we give them a full translation and the document, whether fake or genuine, I dread to think what they will do."

Jake punched empty air in frustration. "They have weapons and the woman with the knife looks and sounds crazy. My God, she threatened to slit Kristy's cheeks open from mouth to each ear. I'm certain she's the one we kept seeing around in different disguises."

"Jake, I agree," Max continued. "We have no choice in this matter. I would dearly love to meet this bishop and see what role he has in all this and how he became entangled with these lunatics. It doesn't make any sense right now. We need to plan some sort of escape, and preferably with the papyrus. I guess in the right hands it is worth a fortune. We can't make any plans until we know where they are and what is happening. Then maybe it will become clearer. All I can say is that without the papyrus, all our work would be for nothing. I'll be damned if I'm going to surrender it that easily."

Ignatius's feeling of uneasiness persisted. Three days had passed and not a thing had been reported back to him. He decided it was time to put pressure on them all. He reached for his phone. After four or five rings he heard Croxley

THE MAGDALENE MISSION

answer.

"Bishop. What can I do for you?"

Ignatius replied, "I need to see you urgently. Not here, but where you are."

"Why, what's wrong, Bishop?"

"This is taking far too long. I need to see you and evaluate where we are at this point in time. What can you tell me right now?"

There was a long pause.

"Bishop, come to me in three days' time. We can give you an update and show you what we have achieved. Here is our address." He gave it precisely until Ignatius had it all written down. "We look forward to seeing you, Bishop."

He powered down his phone.

Croxley wasted no time calling Max. He got an immediate update on what they had found and where they were in the translation.

"Get here three days from now with everything you have and play no tricks, or you know what will happen. Here is the address you are to go to." He read it. "Is that understood?"

"Understood. Where are our two women? They had better not be harmed."

"I'll help put you out of your misery," Croxley retorted. He snapped his fingers and Bull Morello grabbed Isabella by her ponytail and hauled her, crying out in pain, over to Croxley.

"Keep hold of her, Bull." He then spoke to Max. "You getting this, Doc? You can hear her now. Speak, bitch, speak to your lover." He held the phone to her mouth as Bull jabbed her hard on the sensitive soft spot beneath her ear.

Max and Jake heard her yell of pain.

"You bastard!" Max shouted. "Bella! Bella! Are you harmed?"

She managed to reply with a fearful tone in her voice. "Max, Max, I'm okay, but for how much longer I don't know. Please, do as he ask and for our sakes… do nothing stupid—" The phone was snatched away from her mouth.

"Sensible woman, your professor, Doc. Just do as she asks and the better her and the other one's chances will be. I'm sure I don't need to remind you of how skilled my companions are."

"We'll be there. Please don't harm them."

He never got a reply before the phone was switched off.

Chapter 33

Three Days Later

The bishop decided to arrive mid-morning at the given address. His instructions were clear and precise, and he had little difficulty in finding it. He did not know what to expect but he knew what line of attack he was going to take – funding and the lack of results. Why was it all taking so long? He wanted positive answers, and he wanted them fast. He also didn't know the true situation with the researchers or if there was a sting about to happen – and, if so, would he be a victim? He barely gave the other vehicle parked in the driveway a second look.

Max and Jake had decided to travel together. They felt safer as a pair and Bella and Kristy would be reassured by both of them being present. With mutual trepidation, they approached the front door. It opened before they reached it. Standing there with a pistol pointed in their direction was the

KEN FRY

menacing figure of Marco 'Bull' Morello.

"Okay, you two girlies," he sneered at them, with emphasis on his *girlies* jibe, "walk four paces apart and do exactly as I tell you. Walk straight ahead and when I say stop, you do exactly that and nothing else. Stare straight ahead, now, and get going."

They moved forward until a large double door soon confronted them.

"Stop right there," Bull shouted.

They did exactly that.

The doors slowly swung open as if by magic, revealing a Hispanic-looking woman clad in a tight-fitting bloodred yoga outfit. She had a wide black belt strapped around her waist, from which hung an assortment of sheathed knives and scalpel blades. Around from her neck was a simple, plain gold pectoral crucifix.

"Welcome, my disgusting sinners." She waved a titanium blade close to their faces. "I'll take what you are holding." She took the scroll tube and the bound notes both men were carrying. "Now follow me and no tricks. There's a gun pointing at both of you, and you don't want me to start demonstrating my knife skills. That would be fatal."

A fear of knives had always been one of Max's traits. He felt his heart rate pick up at the thought of it.

At a brisk pace they entered another brightly lit room, the walls hung with what oddly appeared to be highly expensive Polynesian war weapons, spears of varying lengths, and assorted war clubs. Clearly somebody had a lot of money.

Max thought that they could be used in an emergency. At the far end stood a large wooden desk. Seated behind it was Croxley. There was no attempt to disguise his face.

Alexa moved to his side and handed him what she was

carrying. "This is it. That's all they have."

Lifting his head, Croxley allowed a sardonic smile to cross his thin face as his form of welcome. He placed both scroll and notes to one side, making no endeavour to examine the findings. "Sit in those two chairs." He pointed to two that were placed a way back from the desk. "My colleagues are covering you both. You see, no matter what you may think of us, this is clear proof that God is on our side. Before you say anything, I expect you're wondering about your ladies. No need to worry. They are safe here and you will see them soon." With a relaxed gesture accompanied by a soft sigh, he leant back in his chair.

Max spoke, aware that what he was about to say would sound lame. "I just hope they are. They've done nothing to harm you. We want to see them now. We've done what you've asked, and you haven't even looked at it. Why not?"

"All in good time, Doctor Franklin, but I am expecting another visitor and I want him to examine your work. I don't possess language skills and wouldn't truly know if what you have written down is accurate or not, or if you're playing games with us. He won't be long now. Be patient. What I will do is peruse your translation into English." He indicated the large, bulky white envelope.

"That's it," Max replied. "Open it and see. I assure you it's accurate to the best of my abilities."

Before Croxley attempted to read the notes, there was a very loud knock on the outside door.

"It must be him now. He knows you, Alexa, so please answer it, and Bull, keep these two covered."

Like a red ghost, she slid from the room.

Croxley said nothing else but opened a drawer, removed an ugly looking black pistol, and placed it prominently on the desktop.

Soon Alexa returned, leading a portly man attired in the clothes of a Roman Catholic bishop. His florid face showed that he was confused by what he was looking at.

His expectations had been vague, but this exceeded them all.

Croxley rose from his seat. "Ah, Bishop Ignatius, we meet again. How nice of you to visit us. Take a seat and let me explain."

"What's going on here, Croxley, and who are these two people?" He pointed at Jake and Max.

"It's a long story as you know, Bishop. The man holding the gun you have met once before. He is my trusted colleague, Mr Marco 'Bull' Morello. You met in Rome. And this is Ms Alexa Heléne, who you met in various locations, I know. The other two are researchers for the unbelievers. We also hold their two sin-soaked women."

Max glanced at Jake. The language being used helped put the missing pieces of the jigsaw into place. It had, in a few sentences, cleared away much of the fog. They were all religious extremists. What was a Catholic dignitary doing mixing with these sorts of people? Why?

Croxley continued. "Bishop, be prepared to see what these people have found and translated. I know you have some expertise in linguistics." He tapped the cardboard tube. "Here's what you have sought and this man's translation of the missing pages of the so-called gospel of that whore, Mary Magdalene. Satan works in devious ways indeed, you must agree."

Ignatius's eyes opened wide. "Indeed, Mr Croxley, I agree. This is excellent news and far better than I anticipated. Let me look now at both. I should soon be able to tell you something."

"By all means, Bishop, look you may."

Ignatius paused for a moment. Something in Croxley's words gave him a feeling of uncertainty. He reached forward, took the tube, and with great care proceeded to open it. Once revealed, he carefully spread it open across the desk. It was then that he saw Croxley's gun in front of him. Never since the bishop had a near fall from a cliff face when he was a young boy, had he experienced real fear. That feeling now reappeared. It was a never-to-be-forgotten experience. There was something wrong here. Bottling down that feeling, he refocused on the papyrus. An immediate impression formed. *This is remarkable. The condition is hard to accept, but I believe it is genuine.*

The room went quiet, all eyes on the bishop as he scanned the papyrus and turned his attention to the text. This was a more difficult task.

He looked up. "The inks need examination for time-period authenticity. What was used in those days bears no relation to modern inks and fluids and if genuine, it would be difficult to find anywhere in this day and age. I can make out certain words. Let me see the translation."

Not saying a word, Croxley handed it to him.

He peered at it and then went back to the manuscript. "It all looks remarkably genuine, but I need to read it closely and compare the two. I will take them with me."

"I don't think so, Bishop. These items are our possessions and safeguards. We will protect and look after them as long as needed. Any examination will be done only with my permission. I need to think that over, and other possible options." He tapped the pistol several times.

The implications were becoming clearer to the bishop. His

fears were hardening. Nervousness was etched into his faltering voice. "But Mr Croxley, we have funded this entire operation. These items are surely ours. Is that not so?"

In reply, Croxley picked up the pistol and twirled it lazily around his fingers. "My dear bishop, we have a childish saying where I come from, and it often proves true. Would you like to hear it?"

"What is that?"

"It is simple and even the members of your church, with all their stolen foreign art and treasures, would understand it. It simply states," he paused for effect, *"finders keepers."* Croxley smiled at a puzzled-looking Bishop. "As I said... simple, isn't it?"

Ignatius found courage. "You can't get away with this, Croxley. It looks like once a thief always a thief. I want these items. We paid for them to preserve the true teachings of Christ and you and your church agreed, and we made a deal that these scurrilous words and teachings should be destroyed before any museum got its hands on them. Did we not?"

Croxley ignored him and turned to Alexa Heléne. "Alexa, my wonderful found daughter. Bring in the two women. Bull and I have weapons enough to deter any moves from these two, and also our wonderful bishop here. Bring them to us."

Two pistol barrels trained on the three seated men.

"What is it you want, Mr Croxley?" Ignatius asked cautiously. "More money? If so, there's none."

"Well, well, a Roman Catholic churchman lying. Hard to believe, eh? Tell me something, Bishop... does your pope know *exactly* what you are up to? I think perhaps he should."

"You wouldn't dare!"

"Try me and see."

THE MAGDALENE MISSION

The bishop struggled for composure. "What is it you want? You are a man of God, or so I believed. You want these falsehoods and lies destroyed as much as we do, or so you said. What are you trying to do?"

"I had to think hard about that, Bishop. You see, God loves me, and he governs my every action. He believes what I do will help spread his word – more so than all of your meaningless parrot-like Masses. I am the sword in his hand. Every word I speak is by and for him. I do no wrong!"

The bishop replied, "Satan has won you over. I can only guess you want more money?"

Not a word was spoken. The silence was broken only by the door opening as a knife-wielding Alexa roughly pushed in the two distraught women.

Max and Jake sprang to their feet.

Croxley's shout stopped them making another move. "Sit back down. You were not given permission to move."

Bella and Kristy, both in tears, rushed to their men and held them tight.

Alexa moved to separate them.

"Let them be," Croxley sharply commanded. "I enjoy watching emotional scenes, as I'm never likely to personally encounter one. The only thing that exceeds that enjoyment is having my God's Chosen Evangelist Church's funds expand. What we have earned from this bishop in front of us has been substantial but nowhere near enough to cover the amount of trouble we've had to endure on this mission. Besides, we will need further funding for other projects I have in mind. Another two million dollars should, I think, cover my needs. What say you, Bishop? Just put yourself in your pope's place and consider what he would think of your little enterprise. Laicization is a very strong possibility, don't you think? Just think of the delightful meal the media would make of it."

Ignatius's florid face paled. Here had arisen a situation he had not foreseen or planned for. As he looked at the four prisoners, he assumed they had no idea what they had embraced.

He was wrong.

The researchers had got it right but had become pawns on Croxley's chessboard.

Max was desperately attempting to work out how they could escape and take the scroll with them. The notes and translation were not so important, as he had made several copies on his laptop under a variety of different file names. He looked across to Croxley. "The bishop is correct. A positive ink analysis would be a large step in proving the authenticity of the manuscript, and at the same time, the papyrus could be checked. The circumstances surrounding this find were unprecedented and truly amazing." Max had caught their complete attention and Croxley had seen only part of the evidence himself.

He went on to explain the train of events that led them to the Orthodox church in Brookwood, including the death of Jacques de Molay and finding his heart as intact as if it had been just removed from his living body in early medieval times.

The whole time he was saying all this, his brain was in top gear trying to find a way out of their predicament and save the evidence. He had to play for time, and he knew his comrades would understand totally what he was doing. They had all known him long enough.

"You mean," cut in Croxley, "this could be a fake? How much more of this is fake – and that includes the rubbish in the Berlin Museum?"

THE MAGDALENE MISSION

Max knew he'd gained ground and he got into full flow. He turned to the bishop. "Bishop, Mr Croxley has it all in his possession. I don't think that's likely to change. Frankly, we don't give a fig what the two of you agreed. Our brief was to trace its whereabouts and if found make of it what we could and then present it and our findings to our sponsors for more detailed examination. Should you be wondering, we of Professor Vanton's team are each acknowledged experts in our fields of research. You are correct, Bishop. A positive ink and papyrus test would confirm its authenticity and age. Whether Magdalene wrote it, or if Christ was a Buddhist monk, is entirely an open question and not ours to answer. Arguments, no doubt, will rage on."

Both Croxley and Ignatius listened intently, then Croxley spoke. "I think not, Doctor Franklin. You see, there will be no arguments at all, as we intend for this blasphemous trash to be destroyed. But we're prepared to be flexible if the price is right."

"If you want to destroy it, why don't you two destroy it now and save us the bother of more work? There's little more that we can do apart from going through it all over again and analysing the ink and papyrus. I can get this done for you in just a few days. The nearest, most suitable location would be Surrey University, not far from here. I'm well known there and at one time, headed their chemical and historic testing facilities. It should not be difficult to do. For you, Mr Croxley, that should be attractive, and there would be no risk of you losing it, and then you can increase the bid once it's been verified."

"To answer your questions, Doctor, I am intensely curious about what you have found and what sort of people are so easily fooled by this rubbish. I may consider your offer, but please read to me, firstly, an extract or two – a few lines would be sufficient. I'm sure our bishop would like to hear also."

The bishop nodded assertively.

Croxley picked up the notes and turned to a querulous-looking Isabella. "Professor, please read aloud so we may all hear." He passed the large envelope across.

Isabella looked at Max, who gave her a reassuring look, telling her it was okay.

"Pick any place you like, Bella. I can guarantee they will not have heard anything like it. I found it astonishing."

She clearly gulped, and attentively scoured what he had translated. She saw a piece that seemed difficult to understand and slowly began to read it aloud.

"And Issa did command me to tell you what I know to be true as he told me. All our teachers have learnt this basic truth. Preserve well. The white snow may fall upon the silver plate as the snowy heron in the bright moon hides. You may ask yourselves what sort of faith must we have? There are four. The first is faith in God. From this will arise joy in your hearts and your prayers. The second is faith in me, and all those who were before my time, but had knowledge of God, as do I. The third is great faith in my words and my teachings. From this your understanding of me, and of my place in this universe, will give rise to the fourth faith. The fourth is that you will establish a community of adherents who will look upon my words and they too will grow in faith and wonderment at the natural structure and of me, and all those who came before me. You have a torch in your hand now that you have passed the dark night of the soul. This gives to you the power of fire and the light to see through the darkness ..."

"Stop right there." Ignatius looked flushed and angry. "I have no need to hear more. It's a load of mystical Eastern-style rubbish." He turned to Max. "Is the rest of it along this theme?"

THE MAGDALENE MISSION

"Mostly, I would say. All ten pages," Max replied. "It is Mary Magdalene passing on the words of Issa, known in the West as Yeshua or Jesus."

Croxley looked across to Alexa, who had drawn her scalpel. Her face was a mask of indignant fury. "Easy, Alexa. Do not worry, this blasphemous Eastern junk will never be seen by anyone but us and a very wealthy benefactor. Remember, God has summoned us. Everything I do or say is sanctioned by God. We are his warriors, chosen by Him for this sacred task. Now all we need to know is if what we have here is genuine or not." He turned to Ignatius. "This poses a problem, does it not, Bishop? Should it prove to be genuine, I might – just *might* – consider passing it on to you for another two million dollars and then you may take it back to Rome and no doubt bury it somewhere in the Vatican vaults for the rest of eternity. There could be many very wealthy bidders for a document of this quality. My church was chosen by God to find this garbage. I've no fear of letting it fall into your hands, for I know you would never publish it. Yet money is a very powerful persuader. It is true, God may wish my church to profit from its sale and he seems to be thinking that way. However, if it fails clinical testing, the original may exist elsewhere, and museums and other unbelievers, like these here, will search for it forever. So… let's hope it proves to be genuine, for all our sakes."

"Well, what do you want me to do next?" Max asked.

"You could easily trick us, Doctor. Just how long would you be?"

"Two or three days, at the most."

"We can live with that, and you will not go alone. To ensure our interests, our esteemed bishop will accompany you at all times. Your three colleagues will remain with us.

Any attempts at deception and they will be the first to suffer the consequences."

"Now, just a minute." Ignatius stood up. "I'm not having this. *Gesù Santo!*"

"You have little choice, Bishop. Refusal will mean you'll never know what these people have found, and you'll have lost a lot of money with nothing to show for it. What's it going to be?"

Ignatius slumped back in his chair. An expression of defeat crossed his face. He was cornered and had underestimated his erstwhile partner. "Very well, I'll do it."

"Wise decision, Bishop." He turned to Max. "No harm will come to your friends here. Take the papyrus and be on your way. We'll wait for your return and we're hopeful for a successful outcome."

Max took the tube and with a concerned expression, spoke to his colleagues. "You have his promise that you will be safe. Don't do anything rash to provoke them. They are highly dangerous, as you know. I will be back as soon as I can." He embraced each of them. "Bishop, come with me. We will travel in separate cars, so follow me closely." The last thing Max wanted was the bishop sitting next to him and asking stupid questions and making various observations and comments.

CHAPTER 34

The University of Surrey
Guildford

Max's arrival, along with his guest, was expected. Max was almost an honoured figure there and full arrangements had been made for his requirements. Arrangements had also been made for overnight stays as long as was needed.

Max made certain that everyone knew who Ignatius was and his interest in the find. Amongst the technicians and researchers there arose considerable interest in Max's discovery, especially interpretation of the language and testing both the inks and papyrus. The scroll was causing excitement amongst various departments, with many people anxious to get a glimpse of it.

They got to work on it at once, and C-14 testing was first on the list.

The bishop was impressed and did not doubt the quality of investigation. Max appeared to know most of the investigators and to be held in high esteem.

The bishop, for once, felt out of his depth and was

overcome by the need for prayer. He was directed to the Centre for Religious Life and Belief. It was also known as the Quiet Centre. He was going to beseech God to ensure this hideous piece of work would never truly see the light of day and never to be published. It was an affront to all that he had ever believed in. It was the work of Satan, yet even the pope had accepted it and Magdalene's role in the church's structure. He prayed also for Croxley and for another two million dollars to give the man. If not, who knew what Croxley's next move would be? He no longer trusted him and was regretting his choice of a former criminal. He sat in prayer for an hour, awaiting an answer.

Deep silence.

Stillness.

He thought he heard a soft whisper. His prayer was being answered.

He offered his choices.

There was clear approval of one – to burn or destroy the heretical rubbish as soon and as quickly as possible.

Saranno fatti… thy will be done. To destroy it meant he had to get hold of it and so far, he had not been able to properly do so. Now he had to seize an unguarded moment or end up paying the money demanded. *How am I to do that?* Slowly, an idea began to form. It was a risky proposition and could end with deaths, including his own. If so, then so be it. His reward would be great in heaven. Was he not a favoured one and had he not been chosen for this awesome task? *Come what may, I will endure to the bitter end, if need be.*

With joy in his heart, he arose from his prayers. Indeed, it was a marvel that God had spoken to him and him alone. He knew what he must do and how to play the game as best he was able. He strode back to the research facility. He could do

THE MAGDALENE MISSION

little more than wait.

Max had been given a preliminary report on both ink and papyrus. As he suspected, the early C-14 test findings looked promising. There was every sign that both materials were of genuine origin. It was at that moment the bishop walked in, looking uncertain.

"Bishop, you look troubled. Well, here is some good news that may give you some cheer. The early tests appear favourable and they indicate the gospel to be genuine. In every department."

The bishop wasn't certain that was the news that he wanted to hear, and it sent him into a coughing bout. He spluttered a reply. "Doctor Franklin, it is not a gospel, it is a fabrication by enemies of our church."

"Science says otherwise, Bishop. A small snippet was removed from a corner for a deeper analysis, and you are at liberty to read the early report. My translation is also being worked on and I am waiting to see what results they find." He handed him the initial translation notes, which barely differed from his own.

The first lines the bishop read stated clearly and simply:

"Let us debate this". Yeshua has said to me. "Magdalene, you are undergoing great change. Something is dying in you and you are a new person with the wisdom of a thousand Solomons. The dark night of the soul will pass from you, for you and all preparing for my shining light. God my Parent's wisdom from heaven is like the forging of metal. Through this and through me you will be stronger in a way not known before. With faith in God who is in your heart,

you may come to know that God is neither male nor female."

Oh disciples, Yeshua has said these things to me that I may tell you. Know that what is before your face and then what is hidden from you will be disclosed through me and that which is buried will be risen...

Ignatius's face expressed his anger and fury at such words. He read no further. *"Tutta spazzatura.* Utter rubbish! It is preposterous. Christ would not have spoken like that and certainly not to a woman many believe had a history of whoredom. Christ's disciples were all male and that's the way the church keeps its priests and hierarchy. I hope and pray our pope keeps it that way."

"Well, that's your problem, Bishop. I want nothing to do with any of it. I deal in scientific facts and not fairy stories like virgin births, rising from the dead, and heavenly ascensions. Interesting, don't you think, that you can believe the likes of that, but when real evidence appears... you automatically reject it? As I said, that's your problem and not mine. Control your anger and know that you have diligently watched over me and know I am not pulling any tricks. The initial ink testing has been completed and it is in keeping with the ancient time period. It is a mixture of soot, probably from a cooking pot, and a resin composite. It's spot-on, Bishop. The papyrus dates from the same era. Whatever, you will reject it as rubbish because it derails your fairyland belief system. Let's see, eh?"

Ignatius knew he had another immediate problem and that was Croxley. The document was looking genuine enough for the man to demand another two million dollars, or maybe sell to a higher bidder. Yet didn't he want to destroy it – or was that all a bluff to get as much money from him? He knew something had to be done and he slowly had an idea of what

THE MAGDALENE MISSION

he might do to save two million dollars and leave no trace of these missing ten pages. If successful, it would all be over and done with, and true Catholicism would be saved from Satan.

Three Days Later

It was midday when the final and complete results were handed to Max, together with a round of applause from excited researchers. He was warmly congratulated on his discovery and the work he'd put into the translation. They told him it was extremely accurate and an extraordinary piece of work, and possibly of major importance.

The bishop scowled and abstained from any applause.

The written report confirmed all of Max's findings and intuitions. He was correct on every point.

An hour later, they were driving back to Croxley and the captives. Max's brain was working overtime on what their next move could be. He wasn't coming up with any answers. Croxley and his other two lunatics were dangerously armed, and he had no solution for that. He sensed the bishop mistrusted Croxley and his demands and insinuations. Maybe there could be an opening there, but there was no way he was going to endanger the lives of his friends with risky behaviour.

The bishop, following close behind, was having similar thoughts. If somehow the papyrus could be destroyed, he wouldn't have to agree to the two million dollars Croxley was demanding. He had a risky plan, but there was no other way.

KEN FRY

For the length of that journey, both men were wrapped in thoughts of how they were going to deal with the situation when they arrived.

Chapter 35

Isabella, Kristy, and Jake were locked in a room that overlooked the front entrance of the house. Every so often, Bull or Alexa, both armed, would check on them.

Bella was depressed. Her once-bright countenance had gone, and she now looked vulnerable and ill at ease. She found the thought of losing their prize – discovered in an amazing manner – unbearable, as she knew the other two did.

"Jake," she said, "there has to be a way out of this, but I don't know what."

"Nor do I, but let's hope Max has thought of one. Knowing him, he will have come up with something."

"Well, here's our chance." Kristy spoke. She was looking out of the window. "He's just come up the drive with that bishop close behind him."

Before they could react, the door swung open and the figure of Bull filled the frame, pointing his gun at them. "Okay, you brain-dead limeys. Out of here and down the stairs. Any crap and you know what I will do."

They didn't argue and made their way downstairs.

KEN FRY

Awaiting them were Croxley and Alexa.

"You three, up against the wall and don't move." Croxley's pistol added emphasis to his command.

They backed up as Alexa went to let the two men in.

Max entered, together with a pensive-looking bishop. Max had a firm grip on the tube and the research documents.

"Welcome back, Doctor Franklin. I hope your trip was successful so that we may all profit from your findings. As you see," he waved his arm at the three researchers against the wall, "your friends are safe and well and no harm has come to them. Now, tell me everything." He waved his gun at him. "I'm all ears."

"Before I start," said Max, "you have what you want and there's little we can do to persuade you not to destroy it or whatever. I've kept my word. Once you have it in your hands, let us go, as you promised. We will not say a word to the police or any authorities. You will be able to bargain with the bishop freely and we will be on our way."

"We shall see, Doctor. We shall see. Now, stop wasting time and start."

"As I guessed, Mr Croxley, everything we found is one hundred percent genuine, and that includes my translation of this section of the gospel. It is intriguing that it is written in Aramaic and not Sahidic Coptic like the rest." Max carefully extracted the papyrus from the tube. "The ink that was used, and the papyrus, are in keeping with the era this was supposedly produced. The entire thing is in the most remarkable condition, considering it was locked in a casket that held the raw heart of a man who was burnt at the stake and believe it or not, that remarkable heart was as fresh as the day the man was killed. I suspect that in some mysterious way, it had much to do with the preservation of this gospel.

THE MAGDALENE MISSION

Especially this sensational missing Aramaic section." Max began to spread out the papyrus across the table.

"Not so fast," the bishop interrupted. "I have severe doubts about the validity of this whole thing, and your translation, Doctor. Let me show you." He elbowed Max away and pulled the papyrus around to himself, bending over at the same time as if to examine it more closely.

His left hand, unseen, reached into the folds of his cassock. He found what he was looking for, the Zippo lighter he'd used many times at Mass and other church services.

He had it out in one swift and practiced movement, expertly flipping it open to produce a hot, flickering flame. "If you people will not destroy this rubbish, then I will. Behold!" He held up the scroll and attempted to light it.

It would not burn.

That was as far as he got.

Alexa's scalpel slit his face open up to the whiteness of his bone.

Blood gushed.

Screams of pain.

At the same time, a bullet from Bull's pistol turned Ignatius's chest into a bloody mess. He slumped backwards, crashing into Croxley's desk before hitting the floor with a heavy thud.

The scroll spun into the air and was caught by an astounded Max. Without hesitation, he whirled around to his companions. "Out, now, and run like mad."

Croxley and the murderers stood there in stunned silence broken only by the groans and moans of a man dying on the floor.

Croxley roared, "You idiots! You've just ruined my chance of getting another two million. Go after them, now. I want that scroll!" He brought his angry fist down hard on the table.

It was a second or two before they reacted. Scurrying from the room, they went in hot pursuit. It was not quick enough. Their prey had escaped and only the sound of a car screeching away remained.

"They've gotten away. We've lost them." Croxley looked furious.

"No, we haven't," Bull replied. "I know where they live."

Croxley ignored Bull's attempt at reassurance. "You idiotic fools. Now we are without a potential source of income. You won't be getting another cent from me."

Bull again explained that he knew where they lived, and they'd handle it.

"All is not lost, then. Let's leave this place. Grab your things. Let's go… now!" Croxley shouted.

"What about that fat shit bleeding on the floor?" Alexa was excited by the sight of blood.

Croxley replied, "Don't worry. He's almost dead. It's been four minutes and his blood is beginning to coagulate. Let's go!"

Chapter 36

Max hit the accelerator as hard as he could, and the car hurtled up past eighty miles per hour in swift time.

"We got away, and with the scroll and the translation. We have not failed yet." Isabella was jubilant.

"Don't get carried away." Kristy looked afraid. "They know where I live. We can't go back there. They'll find us."

"What about the bishop? I guess he's dead," Jake offered.

Max answered, "He's done for, and I bet they won't be hanging around to see if he can recover, which I guess is most unlikely."

"Where do we go?" Jake asked.

"My place in London," Isabella suggested. "It's quiet and out of the way in Saint John's Wood. Max, go for it."

After several minutes of silence, Max asked, "Why didn't it burn?"

"I've no idea," Isabella answered. "This whole thing gets weirder by the minute. We discover an almost-beating heart looking as fresh as a patient's on an operating table, lying next to Magdalene's gospel, looking as if it had been written yesterday, both in a shiny gold casket that's been around for centuries."

"Don't forget," Kristy added, "it wasn't just any old heart, it was that of Jacques de Molay, the Grand Master of the Templars. Their beloved and patron saint was Mary Magdalene, not Mother Mary. They practically worshiped her. The missing pages from her gospel had been placed next to his heart, and this might sound crazy, but it seems as if they were guarding each other. Why would it not burn? Hell, those Zippo lighters burnt down entire villages in the Vietnam War. Why not a simple, fragile piece of work like the papyrus?"

"This may sound even stranger," admitted Isabella. "I don't hold with bizarre or fanciful theories, but I have one here. What if she wants the world to know the deeper insights of Yeshua and herself? From what we have seen, they go far beyond the rudimentary Judeo-Christian thoughts and teachings. She wants to be saved and refused to burn. We have become its guardians."

Max kept driving as fast as he dared. He managed a comment. "What a load of rubbish, Bella, and coming from you, of all people." He steered the car in the direction of London. "This crap has to stop. We are undoubtedly in a mess and in some form of danger. We could take the easy route out of this and let them have what they want, or we could hang on to it and deliver it to our backers."

"Easier said than done," replied Bella. "They know where to find us from our phones and addresses. We cannot stay in one place for more than twenty-four hours. We have to keep moving, and going back to Berlin and the museum might be a good idea."

"Remember," added Max, "it is not ours. It belongs to the Orthodox church in Brookwood Cemetery, and the abbot. We made him a promise and before we do anything, we need his permission. I intend to honour that promise. Any of you disagree?"

For a few moments there was silence, then Bella spoke. "As leader of this venture, I agree. We'll spend the night at my place and then tomorrow we go back to Brookwood and honour our obligations."

The District of St John's Wood
London NW8

Isabella's house was almost hidden in a secluded construction of Georgian architecture. Max had stayed there many times. The interior was spacious and surprisingly decorated, with chandeliers, fireplaces, Victorian Chesterfield sofas, and heavy floral drapes and curtains. A mixture of oil and watercolour paintings adorned the walls. She lived in some style.

As a precaution, they parked away from the house and drew the curtains. They double locked and bolted the doors and turned the lights down low. If they were attacked, any of Isabella's neighbours would hear the gunshots and the police would arrive in double-time, fully armed.

Their nervous conversation ranged over recent events and what they could say to the abbot, and if he would be prepared to deal and meet with their sponsors.

"Shouldn't we be reporting the suspected death of Bishop Ignatius?" Kristy asked.

"Not a chance," Max responded. "He was as bad as Croxley and the others. Croxley will go into hiding while he's hunting for us. I guarantee that our fate will not be pleasant if they find us. That mad witch with the knife is one scary horror. The way she slashed open the bishop was from your worst nightmares. I would not want to be alone with her anywhere."

"So now we know that they're extreme religious lunatics who apparently will stop at nothing to get their way. 'Thou shalt not kill' is something they choose to ignore, seeing themselves as God's chosen and sanctioned warriors."

"Well, anyway, tomorrow we will be in Brookwood. It should be safer there and they'll have no idea where we are." Jake sounded optimistic.

It was then that Bella's spare phone sent a text alert. Apprehensively, she opened it. Her voice trembled as she read it aloud.

Hello, Professor. We found all your other phone numbers on the phone you left behind. We will find you. You can be sure of that. Looking forward to making a mess of your face before you die!

Bella slumped back into her chair, visibly shaking, and feeling an uncontrolled wave of nausea flood through her entire body. "Oh my God! What are we to do?"

Max placed his arm around her. "Switch it off, Bella. They won't find us if we keep moving."

"They seem to know every move we make. How can that be?"

"I've no idea."

"I have." Jake stood up. "We are being tracked and there's only one way they could do that, and that's with a magnetic car listening and tracking device."

"Why didn't we think of that before?" Max said.

THE MAGDALENE MISSION

Jake grabbed the car keys. "Don't even think about that. I'm going to check that car from top to bottom. I might take a while."

"My God." Kristy held Bella's hand. "Let's hope he's right. It could explain everything."

"What do we do with it if he finds it?"

"Easy," said Max, "we smash it to bits!"

Twenty minutes later, Jake appeared, carrying a small black device of some sort. "This is it." His voice was triumphant. "It was affixed behind one of the rear seats, up against the metal backing. Totally concealed unless the seat was stripped. It's recording every conversation and tracking our location. It's still active, and they must know where we are."

Max left briefly and reappeared with a very large hammer, which he clenched in his fist. He used it to smash the device several times with all the force he could muster, reducing it to bits. "It's done for, they no longer know where we're going." He held the hammer aloft. "So, let's get away from here quickly. They must have tracked us this far, but no longer."

"No, let's wait." Bella sounded firmer. "They don't know London, especially this area. Even if they did find the car, they would still have to find us, and that would be like looking for a needle in a haystack. Besides, at this time of night, we have nowhere we can immediately go until tomorrow. Don't you agree?"

Jake answered, "I agree, but don't be surprised if they get close to us, whether or not they got a fix from their last reading. It's not impossible."

Chapter 37

"Something has happened. The signal has gone dead." Alexa checked her earphones. They were functioning as they should. "Nothing wrong with these. They must have found my device. I have a location for the last heading. I can still pinpoint it within twenty-five yards. Damn it!" Alexa looked at Croxley. "What now?"

"Drive to it, as fast as you can. I doubt, if they found it, that will stay there for long. If we lose them, we have no idea where they will be going."

Using the car's built in sat-nav system, Alexa set a fast pace, following the directions shown. It was not long before she was able to navigate to the given location in the St John's Wood area.

"Shit," she muttered, barely audible. "We will never find them in this." She indicated what she was looking at. Parked on each side of the road, cars lined the entire street, almost touching each other in places. There wasn't a gap to be seen.

Croxley spoke. "Just drive slowly along it. I will scan to the left and Bull to the right. Once we reach the end, we'll turn around and repeat the exercise over and over if we have to. If they're here, they'll know we've arrived and would be getting jumpy. So… let's do it nice and slow, as we check for giveaway signs like heads and drapes moving. Do it, Alexa."

She got going, also checking as many cars as she could, but driving made it difficult for her to pinpoint any particular vehicle.

"Keep going until something happens or I tell you to stop," Croxley ordered."

Thirty minutes later, they came to a halt and climbed out of their vehicle before slowly walking along both sides of the street, carefully scanning each house – as much as they dared – from top to bottom.

Their activities had not gone unnoticed. Isabella and her team had kept the lights down low and with the thick net curtains, they were impossible to see from outside. They kept constant watch. A car passing by slowly didn't attract their attention until it returned in the opposite direction, again and again, several times, until they lost count.

"It has to be them," Jake said. "They probably got a fix on our location before Max smashed their tracker."

"Without a doubt," Bella answered. "They have made too many passes at a slow speed, as if they are looking for a clue."

"Look," added Max, "they've stopped. My God, they are getting out! It's them, all right, and they are walking along the pavement. They are looking at every house. Get back from the curtains and out of sight. If they knock, or whatever, we remain silent and hidden."

Kristy paled and looked frightened. "I'm getting scared."

Jake held her tight. "You'll be fine, don't worry."

"Keep out of sight, everybody. We have bolted and double locked the doors and windows. We don't want be shot at again." Max was reassuring and had a natural authority.

They got down on the floor and there they stayed for what seemed an age, remaining silent and straining their ears. They heard nothing further.

Eventually, and with great caution, Max hauled himself up until he was able to look out of the window without being seen. There was nothing there. Their pursuers had vanished. "I think you all can stand up now. It looks as if they've gone. I suggest we all turn in now and set off early in the morning, before seven, for Brookwood."

Chapter 38

Croxley was angry. "That was a complete waste of time. There's no way we're going to find them, and we can't even be sure that this is where they stopped. We couldn't find their vehicle, so God knows where they are. Any thoughts?"

Bull could think of nothing, so he simply shrugged.

Alexa offered her thoughts. "They have been across and throughout the Middle East, plus much of Europe, including Berlin. So where do they eventually end up? In England, of all places. What they were looking for was right in front of them without them even realising it until the goddamned Templars crept into the equation with that weird heart thing and the papyrus, both looking as if they were made yesterday. I know that professor woman made a promise to that creepy abbot guy that she would not do anything before gaining his consent. My guess is we revisit that place and see what's happening. What do you think?"

"I agree." Croxley couldn't think of anything better – nor could Bull, who was looking forward to some gun fun once more.

"Tomorrow, we will pay the place another courtesy visit. Okay?"

There was no other option with the information they had.

Thunderous clouds rolling across the sky, complete with lightning flashes, greeted the team the next morning. It was not going to be a good day. Breakfast was swift and hasty, nothing fried. They had a mission to perform.

Isabella reminded them to be vigilant in all directions and at all times. Their mission, she correctly deduced, was one full of danger and menace, with potentially fatal consequences. Not knowing why, she did an unusual thing. She hugged each team member and kissed them one by one on the cheek. *Somehow*, she thought, *I have to do it*. In her mind there was a compelling urge to thank them all. Without them, the Magdalene would be lost.

Respectful silence followed as they made their way to the vehicle, each wrapped in their own personal hopes and fears.

The journey was going to take the best part of two hours through heavy traffic and lashing rain. Isabella left a message with the abbot to that effect. The rain hammered down as if on a personal vendetta against the mission. They didn't say much during the trip, and they were constantly monitoring what other cars were doing. The weather made it difficult to see clearly, but they saw nothing suspicious or alarming.

Max drove modestly in the conditions and he too was forever checking his rear-view and wing mirrors. He saw nothing to give him cause for worry. "Well, I reckon," he said, "they are going to be doing a lot of guesswork to figure out our next move."

"That's what scares me," Isabella replied in a faltering voice. "It wouldn't take a genius to guess where we might be heading. They know the papyrus belongs to the abbot and his church. It's the first place I'd go looking."

Max answered her grimly, "We don't have much of a choice in this. We made a promise, and we're going to keep it, come what may."

He expertly navigated his way through the thick early morning London traffic before hitting the open road towards Brookwood Cemetery. The rain had stopped and there was now a clearer view. There was still no sign of their trackers.

"We seem to have shaken them off the trail." Jake spoke. "Let's hope it stays that way. I've an idea – while you all negotiate with the abbot or whatever, I will keep watch outside for any sign of them. If there is, I will warn you at once. That way we won't get a nasty surprise like last time."

"I'll go with that," Isabella said. "A smart idea, Jake."

The outlines of the charming abbey and church soon appeared as they drove into the cemetery. The Orthodox church car park was empty. No sooner had they disembarked when Brother Macarius – wearing his habit, its hooded cowl pulled up – was standing there waiting for them. He greeted the team cordially. His welcome came complete with a genuine smile of pleasure. They all took turns embracing him with warm hugs. He appeared to have recovered from his injuries, apart from a faint bruising around his mouth.

In response to their concerned enquiries about his wounds, he replied, "Have no worries, I'm fine, and God has taken good care of me. Come, follow me to Abbot Gregory's rooms. He is well and very much looking forward to seeing you all again."

Striding purposefully, he guided them through the abbey, then respectfully knocked on the abbot's small, dark oak door. They didn't have long to wait before it swung open, and Abbot Gregory stood before them. There was not a mark on him from his previous trauma.

His dour countenance lit up like a Christmas tree when he saw them. His smile broke like sunrise over a dark, forbidden moor. "My dear friends, I thank God that all of you are safe and well. I've prayed for you all, every day. You must tell me all – and where is your man, Jake? Unharmed, I hope?"

Isabella replied, "He is here, Abbot, but he is keeping watch outside in case we receive unwelcome guests again."

"A very wise move. Do come in and take a seat where you can."

They stepped into his plain and simple room, its simplicity broken only by the numerous icons and several crucifixes adorning his walls.

He turned to Brother Macarius. "Brother, please bring in the tea and biscuits I've prepared. We have no desire to see our guests die of thirst or hunger, do we?"

Macarius scuttled away to another room and quickly reappeared with a sizeable wooden tray on which stood a large black teapot, cups, saucers, plates, milk, and sugar, plus a hefty tin of assorted biscuits. Once the ritual tea pouring and biscuit serving were done, Max outlined all the events that had occurred whilst Kristy and Isabella filled in the details of their ordeal and part of the story. The team was careful to avoid the role Bishop Ignatius played in the events. That would come later.

The abbot spoke. "That's an awful story to hear, and I thank God that you are safe and sound and managed to escape those awful people. May God forgive them. Now I come to the part of your story, Doctor Franklin – how did the translation go? I see you are carrying the cardboard tube – with the papyrus still within, I hope?"

Max gave a small smile, which hid the depth of his feelings. "Yes, Abbot, it has all gone better than I dared hope. I've had both the document and ink analysed by the university's research unit. As fresh and as new as they appear, there can be no doubt that both are faultless in their genuine age. The mystery is, how did that happen? We can't answer that but would like to see Jacques de Molay's heart again to see or find out what else we can – if there's anything else to discover."

"Of course, of course," said the abbot. "That goes without saying. Now, what of your translation?"

"It could not have gone better. I'm going to ask Professor Vanton to read out any extract she likes, and you may see it and make any notes you wish. A copy of my translation is available for you right now and the papyrus is rightfully yours. We will come back to that later. Isabella, please select any place you like and read a short translation."

Isabella carefully unfurled both the papyrus and the translation. Firstly, she surveyed everybody with a serious expression and then scanned Max's work before taking a deep breath and beginning to read his words.

Thus did Magda speak to the others. "Behold, Yeshua has said to me so that you might understand. Now you will become fulfilled. Know well that the force of love and that of desire are well balanced and your route to my Parent is through me. The Way is open, and also the gate. It is wide open to those who believe in me. For those who do not, it will not be possible to pass through. God will be in your hearts when all conditions are understood. Know that there is no difference between the infinitely small and the infinitely large.

They are the same... and you will see, through me, that they do not exist. Know this well and you will see God ..."

Isabella stopped. She was speechless. She carried on reading until she reached the end. There were no interruptions. When she'd finished, she looked up and was unable to prevent an obvious gulp. In some places it was complicated, yet in others it was so simple and beautifully poetic.

The room was held in the grip of silence. The abbot and his monk exchanged meaningful glances.

Max broke the spell. "Well, folks, that was as clear as I could get it. Other translators might vary a bit here and there, but trust me, the complete essence is there. Pretty stunning material, right? God – it is being said – is without gender. That's going to upset a lot of people."

Isabella joined in. "The whole thing is startling. I've never read anything like it in the Bible, or the non-canonical works of Philip and Thomas, either. Or, come to that, any other religious texts. God is seen as a non-gendered source, which Yeshua describes as Parent. Astonishing! Now I see why the Templars venerated the Magdalene so much and why they removed these pieces. They must have known the uproar they would have caused in the patriarchal-dominated church. If this gets into the media, there will be a similar reaction, and our kidnappers were well aware of that. They tried to burn it, but it wouldn't ignite. That, to me, suggests there's still a great mystery around this, and That's the reason I wish to see inside the casket again."

Finally, the abbot spoke. His voice was quiet, low, and solemn. "That was deeply profound. I congratulate you, Doctor Franklin, and you, Professor, and your team. You have discovered something remarkable, which, I am certain, will cause a major storm with Christians across the globe, should it be released. From my own point of view, and that of Brother Macarius, we hold similar opinions on this subject. I found nothing evil or bad about the words of Jesus spoken through his companion the Magdalene that you have read, Professor. It adds substance to my deep beliefs. I found it intensely moving, philosophical, and profoundly reassuring. They are the words of Jesus, of that I am convinced, irrespective of Emperor Constantine and his long line of patriarchal successors." He stood. "Come, let us go to the shrine room, and bring your material with you."

They all followed him back down the way they had come before stepping outside.

Jake was still there and was cordially greeted by the two monks. He was asked to join them but refused.

"No, I don't think so. I am of more use keeping an eye open for unwanted guests than being inside. Forgive me."

"Of course," the abbot replied. "If something occurs, please let us know."

"I will, but I'm hoping it will all be quiet."

The casket remained as they'd last seen it. Nothing had changed and its air of sacred dignity remained. The candles flickered in their gold holders and the smell of frankincense remained strong, lingering in every crevice and cranny. It would always be that way, as long as the monks remained.

Max looked around the casket. This time, there'd be no need for tools to dislodge the large lid. All that was needed was muscle power to move it and slide it away. Brother Macarius and Max himself did what was required.

"One, two, three! Heave and heave again," Max shouted, gritting his teeth.

Inch by inch, the massive wooden lid began to move. It

was easier that time. They kept at it and Brother Macarius, unused to real physical effort, began to drip with sweat.

"One more heave, Brother," a breathless Max encouraged.

Slowly, the lid came away and they were able to lever it upwards and lower it gently to the ground. Everybody moved to the rim and peered into the casket. It looked no different to the way they had left it. Saint Edward's bones were as they had been, wrapped in a heavy shroud, unchangingly resistant to the relentless wheel of time. The smaller gold casket was also as they had left it, complete with its replaced bitumen seal, which Max again, using his special knife, began to strip away. This time, only a slight trace arose of the wondrous scent that had escaped before. Still wrapped in the purple cloth was Jacques de Molay's heart.

Both the abbot and Brother Macarius knelt, as before, with heads bent low and murmuring prayers, complete with several signs of the cross.

Isabella moved to the casket, holding the papyrus she had removed from the tube. She was trembling but looked at Max and nodded.

He understood, with that special understanding that existed between them.

She placed the papyrus next to the wrapped heart.

Intuitively knowing what she wanted, Max gently, and with great care, proceeded to unwrap the heart once more. The last fold came away as everyone present stood transfixed at what was happening… and only guessing at what the meaning might be.

Their mouths dropped open.

The monks once more fell to their knees.

Max reeled backwards.

Kristy began weeping.

Isabella did not budge. She was immoveable. She knew what would happen.

It did.

The papyrus came into contact with the still fresh-looking heart. Two things happened at once. The edge of the papyrus began to flutter. Slowly at first, then quickly picking up speed. It rippled, but never budged from the spot where it was placed. The entire document vibrated with a mesmerising movement.

The heart began to beat.

They were reuniting.

Heart and papyrus beat in rhythmic movement, as one.

Kristy passed out.

Max sat down heavily next to the two stupefied monks.

Only Isabella remained unfazed. What she was witnessing was far beyond anything she had explored or learnt. In her heart and mind was complete acceptance of what was happening there.

She understood.

Parting had been a great, inexplicable sorrow for both heart and papyrus, which no amount of science and explanation could make sense of. They were as one, different but not… united but separate. A complete wholeness. As she gazed in wonderment, the movements slowed and eventually stopped. They once more looked normal, like when they had first seen them.

Not a word was spoken for what seemed an eternity. Bella remained where she stood, still staring at both items. Abbot Gregory and Brother Macarius remained kneeling, still praying. Max helped Kristy to her feet before moving over to Bella, who was now gently weeping. He placed his arm around her and pulled her in close.

She looked up at him. "That really did happen, didn't it?"

He answered, "It did. If I hadn't seen it with my own eyes, I would never have believed it. Bella, it was real. It happened."

Kristy held on to them both with a look of astonishment still on her face. "Jake has missed all this. He will find it hard to believe." She managed a small smile.

Max resealed the small casket, leaving the papyrus where Bella had placed it.

Both monks were now on their feet. Each had a look of stupefaction on his normally serene face.

"God is unbelievable. It is almost hard to believe. We have seen him at work truly for the first time, and close up. We are blessed indeed," the abbot murmured.

"Abbot, we have to get this lid back on. Brother Macarius, can you help, please?"

He did so willingly, and it was much simpler than hauling it off.

Once it was in place, Bella turned to them all. "I had a suspicion something strange was going to happen, and this exceeded my wildest imaginings. Abbot, this presents us with a few problems. Our pursuers are after the papyrus and I fear, if they obtain it, they will sell it to the highest bidder or else attempt to destroy it again. My team and I have another problem that we need to discuss privately concerning our mentors and how we will present this to them and what they will have to say about the situation. May we come back to you in a few days' time if we have concrete proposals?"

"By all means," he replied. "I look forward to what you have to say."

With that agreement, they proceeded back to the car and the ever-vigilant Jake.

"No sign of our stalkers," were his first words. "Hey,

THE MAGDALENE MISSION

what's wrong with you three? You look as if you've seen a ghost."

"You're not far wrong there, Jake. You're never going to believe what we have to tell you, but first it's back to Saint John's Wood."

Chapter 39

Not knowing their destination didn't help Croxley and his hit team. The complexities of London's traffic confused Alexa, who had volunteered to drive, and several times she ended up going in large circles. Eventually, she hit the right route and headed away from London. Soon they were in the county of Surrey and eventually they picked up on a sign for Brookwood Cemetery. It was not long before they arrived, and the St Edward the Martyr Orthodox Church came into view. They drove slowly into the car park, each of them scanning the area, hoping to catch a glimpse of their quarry. There was no sign of them. Unbeknown to them, the birds had flown.

There were a few parked vehicles belonging to church visitors, but they didn't recognise any of them. Some had foreign number plates.

Their car came to a stop, and they clambered out, walking slowly towards the entrance. This time they did without the balaclavas. They were just potential worshippers.

Croxley gave his orders. "Speak to nobody. Let me do that. Watch out for that abbot guy and his monk. If you see them, let me deal with it. Got it?"

"We've got it, Matty," Alexa replied, with a familiarity she rarely used.

They entered the church, attempting to be seen as bona fide worshippers. There were but a few people dotted here and there in pews. Croxley did a double take. A face he recognised was conducting the service. It was that of Abbot Gregory. Gesturing to the other two, he slid into a pew, followed by Bull and Alexa. Behind a closed hand, he whispered, "It's the abbot guy. Let's sit here until he's finished and leave the rest to me."

The service was deeply reverential with the light of a hundred burning candles and bowls of smouldering frankincense placed all around. A figure of Mother Mary, her hand raised in blessing, stood in one alcove. In an opposite alcove, newly added, the red-cloaked and graceful figure of the Magdalene bestowed her blessing to all with a look of kindness.

Alexa was feeling affronted and could not stop the rapid up-and-down movement of her leg and foot.

Bull seemed indifferent.

Croxley, surprisingly, was going along with it all and seemed to be participating with no effort. It was as if he had been there a thousand times before.

Eventually, it came to an end and the abbot made his way to the porch to bid adieu to the worshippers. *'Go in peace'* was his standard farewell. *'And with you'* was the customary response.

Bull and Alexa ignored him, and if she'd had license, she would have gladly slit his satanic throat.

Croxley hung back to ensure he was the last to leave.

Abbot Gregory raised his hand. "Peace be with you, my

son." At the same time, he gave a small smile.

"Thanks, Father," Croxley responded, uncertain of how to address or reply to him. He stood a few paces back to give a signal of non-menace in every way. "I wonder if you can help me."

"If I can, I will, most certainly. What is it?"

"I'm Matthew Croxley. I'm a historian and archaeologist from the USA. I'm a little concerned. I was due to meet four of my friends here this morning, but they don't seem to be around. I'm a little later than intended, but it was a matter concerning Saint Edward and his shrine. Would you know anything of it?"

His name and alleged profession meant nothing to the abbot. He knew nothing of this, and he guessed the professor or Max would have mentioned it. The matter was far too important for such a detail to be overlooked and never mentioned. For some reason he was unable to explain, he felt immediately suspicious. Something was not quite right. The man's voice had a familiar ring to it, but he was uncertain.

He chose to sidestep Croxley's question. "I know nothing of what you ask. You saw the congregation, were not your friends amongst them? Saint Edward's shrine is indeed here, where it has been for many years."

"That my friends are not here is not good news for me. I have no idea how I can contact them, and you have no understanding of whom I'm talking about?"

"None, whatsoever."

Croxley latched on to the idea that the abbot was lying. It was time to try a different approach. "Abbot, I would very much like to see Saint Edward's shrine. I've travelled a very long way to get here from the USA and it was part of my reason for the trip."

THE MAGDALENE MISSION

By now the abbot was on full alert. Something was not right. *How could he have travelled all that way and not be able to connect with his so-called friends? That voice is the same as the intruder's. I'm now almost certain of it.*

The abbot's own voice hardened. "No, you may not. The shrine room is locked and bolted, and visitors are banned for the foreseeable future due to unwelcome guests we had a short while ago. The only people allowed in there will be the police, who will be conducting an on-going investigation with my assistant and myself. Your request is denied, sir."

Croxley noticed at once the change in the abbot's tone and body language, which was reinforced by the arrival of Brother Macarius, who looked concerned.

"Is something wrong, Abbot?"

"I'm not sure, Brother."

There was not much Croxley could do or say but he still had his gun, plus Bull and Alexa. He knew he was going to have to do it the hard way. He had learnt many things in jail, and one was to always challenge and confront your target using every weapon at your disposal.

"I'm going to have to be more persuasive, Abbot." He drew his pistol from behind his back and raised his arm as a signal for the waiting pair standing not too far away. They responded at once and, seeing what was happening, drew their weapons and surrounded the two monks.

Croxley's tone changed. The peaceful, apologetic voice became a menacing snarl. "Now open that goddamned shrine door or both of you risk serious, life-changing injuries."

The abbot knew these people were not messing around, for both he and Brother Macarius had first-hand experience of what they were capable of. "Very well, but there's nothing there that would interest you in any way."

"I'm not so sure about that, Abbot, but we shall soon find out, won't we? Now lead on."

With faltering steps and guns prodding at their backs, they moved reluctantly towards the shrine room. Soon they stood in front of the oak doors. Macarius produced a large metal key from his habit and hesitantly inserted it into the lock. With a low groan, the door swung open and they slowly stepped inside. All was as they had left it earlier. Nothing had changed.

"You know what, Abbot, I don't believe all that crap that you had no idea who my four friends were. Well, they are not my friends, as you well know. We also know they gave you certain promises about that papyrus. They were to return it and talk to you about its eventual destination. We think it's in that damned casket and we are about to find out. So, let's go."

Isabella went rigid and her head jerked. "Stop the car, Max. Stop it, now!" Her voice was as sharp as a new razor, clear and commanding.

"Hey," said Max. "What's wrong, are you okay? What's happened?"

"We have to turn around and go back."

"What are you talking about? What on earth are you saying? Why?"

Both Kristy and Jake had puzzled expressions.

"No, I'm not out of my mind, but you're going to think so after what I'm about to tell you."

"What is that?" Max had an annoyed expression as he brought their vehicle to a halt.

THE MAGDALENE MISSION

"She's in danger."

"Who's in danger? Who is she? What are you on about?"

"The Magdalene. She's in trouble."

"What is this gobbledygook?" Max rolled his eyes.

"She is whispering in my mind. I know it must sound ridiculous, but she is. I can clearly hear her."

"Okay, Bella, we will do as you ask. But if we find nothing, the first thing you do when we get home is see a doctor. I know we all saw something remarkable and unexplainable recently, but this is a step too far. It's way out with the fairies."

Kristy spoke up. "What if it's our nasty kidnappers, what then?"

"We go in armed with our tools." Jake looked more serious than usual. "We still have them all in the car from our last trip. They could prove useful if need be."

"Useless against bullets." Kristy looked nervous.

"Let's not think of that right now," Bella said. "She's calling for our help. Don't ask me anything else. I am a professor and not given to making stupid statements, but I know what I am hearing. Please believe me."

Max broke into a mocking song, "Hi ho! Hi ho! It's off to work we go!" He didn't get much further, as Bella gave him a forgiving slap on his head.

The rest of the journey was spent in an atmosphere of quiet, nervous anticipation. Nobody knew what to expect.

Croxley twirled his gun around his trigger finger as he watched the two monks' faces. They were expressionless and unafraid. He liked that, but no man wants to die. He'd seen hardened villains scream aloud when facing death. These two put them to shame.

"Open the casket." He pointed at it and the two monks.

"We can't." Abbot Gregory spoke evenly. "It's too heavy, and at my age I've no strength left in my body. I'm of little use in such matters. Why don't you use him?" He pointed towards Bull Morello.

"Why I don't is because this is your heretical church's work, and we don't like to sully our blessed hands on Satan's ill-gotten trash. So do try, Mister Abbot, or do you want another beating? If so, it will be harder than last time."

Abbot Gregory was a brave man but did not relish the idea of another savage beating. He nodded at Macarius, who understood and walked to one corner as the abbot went to the other. They tugged together. It didn't move, and the abbot promptly fell to the floor. His face was flushed.

Macarius went to help him to his feet, but Bull beat him to it and rewarded the abbot with a hefty kick, which sent him sprawling back to the ground. Alexa completed the double-hit with another to the ribs.

The abbot groaned and clutched at his chest. He was allowed to stand up.

"We'll give you a couple of minutes to get your breath back and then you try again. Now, you don't want another kicking. If you can't move it, then we might have to smash it open. That would be such a shame to damage your beloved piece of junk, don't you think?" Croxley gave a contemptuous sneer. "Come to think of it, I might just be in the mood to do that, whatever happens here. So come on, my beefy monks, get tugging again. Do it now!" As a gesture of his intent, he smacked the pistol butt hard on top of the casket.

The two monks gasped.

THE MAGDALENE MISSION

"Please don't do that!" Brother Macarius blurted out with an alarmed expression.

The abbot winced and closed his eyes. This was a scene he did not want to watch. He offered up a silent prayer. "Wait, please wait, we will try again."

"What good little boys you are." Croxley turned to Alexa and Bull. "Good guys, aren't they just? Stand by and give them some encouragement if need be."

Both laughed. They knew what he meant.

The two monks got hold of the corners once more. Asking God for strength, they again proceeded to tug and strain at the lid. There was a slight movement from Macarius's corner, but nothing from the abbot's. His prayers were not being answered.

"C'mon, Mister Abbot, put your back into it," Croxley goaded. He winked at Bull. "Bull, give him a helping hand."

Bull didn't need to be asked twice. He knew what was required. It was something he was going to enjoy. As the abbot strained and pulled, Bull's thick fist smashed into the abbot's lower-left side, causing what breath he had left to be lost in one mighty, painful gasp. It sent him sprawling into Brother Macarius, knocking them both to the floor in a tangled heap.

"Oh dear, oh dear!" Croxley shouted.

That went on for a while as very slowly, inch by inch, the bruised monks painfully began to remove the heavy lid.

Chapter 40

The miles passed swiftly by, and all their attention was focused on Isabella, who was sitting, bent low, holding her head in her hands.

Max, unable to keep a hint of sarcasm from his voice, asked, "Are you getting messages from the beyond, somewhere up there, Bella?"

She slowly lifted her head with a strange glint in her eyes. She stared straight out of the windscreen in front of her. She spoke with an uncharacteristic quiet resonance. "Yes, I am. There's danger and we must hurry. She trusts us to do the right thing and knows that we will. We must not take too long getting there or it will be too late." She broke off into a stifled sob.

The way she spoke and the message she gave had a sobering quality about it that shook them all. She wasn't fooling around. Every word of it was deadly serious.

Even Max felt shaken at what she had just said. "Jesus," he whispered quietly to himself. "She means every word of it. This is nuts, but it has got my attention, totally. She would never joke about such a thing. I know her too well."

THE MAGDALENE MISSION

He found his foot pressing harder on the accelerator pedal. He picked up the A322 route to Woking and the village of Pirbright with its access to the Greek Orthodox Church of Saint Edward the Martyr.

Soon, it came into view and Max slowed the vehicle down to a crawl as he trickled into the car park as quietly as possible. It was almost empty, apart from one solitary vehicle. That looked suspicious. For a moment, they sat looking at it. Nobody knew what to say, apart from Isabella.

"It's them. She has told me so."

Max raised an eyebrow, but there was no doubting that he was beginning to believe what she was saying. If Kristy and Jake had any misgivings, they showed none. They trusted her totally.

"It's time to choose our tools." Jake, practical as ever, stepped from their car and lifted the rear boot lid.

There before them was a selection of iron crowbars, spades, and axes. They each made their choice – crowbars were the favourite. Even Kristy, the most nervous of all, seemed to have found a hidden strength as she selected a short-handled, finely sharpened hand axe.

As they stood there, they could hear the monks' daily chanted Greek litany drifting through the air. The chanters had no idea about what was happening in their shrine room.

With great caution and trepidation, they approached its sacred portal. The door was shut. If anybody was inside, their approach had not been heard. They stood there, fully alert, with weapons, ready to enter the room.

Isabella spoke. "She is ready. The time is right. We must go in or tragedy is about to occur."

The door was not locked and swung open easily. They surged in, not knowing what to expect. The scene that greeted them was shocking and unexpected.

Both Abbot Gregory and Brother Macarius, bloody and bruised, were attempting to pull the casket lid off. They were a quarter of the way through, and Bull was punching Macarius around his ears. Croxley and Alexa were laughing close by, and it was clear that the monks could take little more before a tragedy unfolded.

The three invaders stopped immediately. They saw their visitors.

They raised their guns.

"Stop right there!" Croxley shouted, firing a warning shot over Isabella's team at the same time.

They froze where they stood and dropped to the floor. Their weapons were concealed under their bodies. In the uproar of their arrival, those items had not been noticed.

Max gave an urgent and hushed whisper. "Don't move a muscle!"

Croxley brandished his gun, covering them all and barking his orders. "Nobody is to do anything. You two grovelling monks, get down on the floor on your stomachs. Do it now!"

There was no doubting what he was capable of. The monks obeyed.

Croxley turned to Max and the others. "I was wondering if we might see you again. This is going better than I expected. Now, very slowly get up so we can see you better."

"When can I start slicing?" Alexa had an excited, gloating look on her face.

"And I want some target practice." Bull was not going to miss out on the fun.

"Soon, I expect, my good soldiers, but we need that papyrus before we do anything."

Slowly, the four hauled themselves up. Their weapons became visible, apart from Kristy's small axe. She had managed to conceal it under her jacket.

Jake spoke from the side of his mouth. "What are we going to do now?"

Isabella gave a shaky answer. "Pray, I guess."

"Well, well, it looks like our friends meant to do us some harm." He had seen the steel crowbars left on the floor. "We can't be having that, can we, now?" His tone hardened. "Right. You two monks pick up the crowbars and put them in the far corner. The rest of you, pull that lid off. These two weaklings," he gestured at the monks, "they are useless. Be quick about it."

A flurry of solid punches from Bull Morello emphasized his commands.

A scalpel-waving Alexa, only too anxious to inflict pain and agony on somebody, menaced the two ladies.

Both Bella and Kristy stood rigid, not daring to move a muscle.

Bull made it clear with his gun what would happen if they tried anything using the crowbars.

Jake and Max each grabbed a corner and did their best to ignore the punches. Bull was enjoying himself. Doing what was ordered, they each heaved at the lid. It moved slightly.

"That's more like it." Croxley smiled. He peered into the casket to see what he was after, but more of the lid needed to be moved before the smaller container could be seen.

Alexa began a demonstration of her blade skills. She placed her hand flat on a nearby surface. With her fingers spread open wide, she began stabbing the gaps between them with increasing speed. It was a flurry of movement, and she did not miss once. It was an impressively scary display of what she was capable of.

Max and Jake continued hauling at the lid, which begrudgingly moved a fraction at a time.

Croxley was becoming impatient and began tapping his pistol butt on the polished top.

Bull was still playing the role of a slave master and kept punching, shouting, cursing, and swearing at the two men.

The lid was now halfway open.

The two of them pausing for breath only gave Bull cause for further abuse.

Watching close by, the monks could do nothing but pray.

Max looked over to Bella and was surprised to see her standing straight and unafraid with a strangely composed expression on her face. It was as if she knew something the others didn't.

"Keep at it," Croxley roared. "No slacking, or it will be the worse for you both."

Jake and Max looked at one another, covered in dripping sweat, before each gave one loud grunt and a final heave at the lid. This time it slid away and fell, standing almost upright, at the bottom end of the casket.

For several long moments, there was complete silence in the shrine room.

"At last," Croxley said with an air of triumph. He moved rapidly to the opening and peered in. The shroud was still there, untouched. The small gold container was close by, and he could see it clearly. It looked no different from when they had last seen it.

Max looked disappointed. *What was Bella going on about? I was expecting something to amaze me, but nothing. It looks the same as it did during our last visit. If we get out of this, she is definitely going to a doctor.*

Croxley reached out and got a grip on the gold container,

THE MAGDALENE MISSION

pulling it towards him.

Alexa spoke to Bull. "I hope he doesn't take too long. I want to get slicing."

"My fists need a rest," Bull added. "My trigger finger is itchy."

Croxley began dismantling the seal around the box.

Bella spoke. "Please, don't touch it. I beg you."

"You're talking crap, lady. I haven't come all this way to go home empty handed. One more outburst and I will tell my soldiers to take good care of you before setting them on your friends. So shut up!"

With that, the seal fell away, and he began to move the top. Soon it was completely off and before him was the heart, wrapped in its purple covering. Next to it was the papyrus he so desperately wanted.

All eyes were fixed on Croxley.

Bella closed her eyes. *Were we too late?*

Croxley stood back and gazed at what he had been seeking. "This is it, folks." At that, he reached for the heart and pulled open the purple-cloth-wrapped bundle. From sheer curiosity, he needed just to look at it. And there it was, looking as fresh and warm as if it had only been put there minutes ago.

"Sweet Christ!" He reeled backwards, looking away, with an expression of utter disbelief.

"What's wrong?" Alexa moved quickly toward him. "Matthew, what's wrong?"

"The damned thing pulsated. I swear it did!"

Alexa stared at it. The heart was motionless. "You must be seeing things. It's dead as a dodo. Look again."

Reluctantly, a shaken Croxley forced himself to glance at the heart a second time. She was right. It was still and quiet.

Bella turned to her team. "We are not too late. She thanks us, and there's more to come. Believe me."

Kristy believed her totally, but the men were not so sure.

Croxley regained his composure. "The damned thing looked so real I guess I hallucinated for a moment." He turned his attention to the papyrus.

Alexa moved back to guard the women. It seemed nothing could faze her. She still held her scalpel, waiting for the time she could use it.

Croxley went to unravel the papyrus from its protective tube.

As he did so, Jacques de Molay's uncovered heart awoke once more. Imperceptibly at first, it began to beat with a steady rhythm, which increased in tempo as it majestically arose into the air to hover over the open casket.

All could see it.

It moved in perfect rhythm.

As if in response, a voice emerged from the papyrus. It was soft, gentle, and full of the milk of elevated kindness. With this appeared an ethereal figure. It was a woman dressed in red robes extending her hands towards the astonished watchers.

"Oh, my Good God," Max blurted, in disbelief at what he was seeing.

Croxley and his troops were in stunned shock. This was no illusion.

A white-faced Bull Morello fired a shot, but it had no effect. It passed through the vision as empty air.

Jacques de Molay's heart continued its rhythmic and pulsating beat. Blood spurted from it from an unseen and unknown source. Not a drop fell to the ground. It re-entered the living organ for all to see.

THE MAGDALENE MISSION

The monks were on their knees and praying with all their might.

Croxley emptied his weapon at both the vision and the beating heart, but his bullets were useless. He kept firing into the air all around him until he ran out of ammunition.

Alexa had not lost total composure, nor was she in any state of shock or disbelief. She shouted at Croxley, "Matthew, it's the work of Satan. It can't harm us if we refuse to allow it. Get up and fight!"

Croxley was stunned and could barely stand, but his faith in Alexa never wavered. He attempted to get upright.

Bull reluctantly tried to join him.

"I'll show you what I can do. Watch!" She moved closer to the ladies, who were standing close together, watching in amazement at what was unfolding. She produced another titanium scalpel. "Which one of you two devil worshippers is first?" She waved it at Bella, who shrank away.

Alexa was totally unprepared for what happened next.

Kristy had allowed her small axe to drop from inside her jacket, unseen, into her hand. It had been overlooked. She had no time for thought. It had to be done at once.

Alexa's hand was outstretched with the scalpel, ready for a swooping slice at Bella's face. It never got there. Kristy gave an almighty yell and brought the axe down hard across Alexa's wrist. There was an agonised shriek of unbelievable pain. Her hand was sliced clean off. It fell to the floor, still clutching the scalpel.

Blood gushing everywhere, Alexa collapsed to the floor, screaming in agony. Her murderous days had come to a savage end.

Both Croxley and Bull went to grab Kristy but were unable to move a muscle. An unseen force prevented them from being able to physically react in any way. Not a finger or muscle obeyed their commands. They were frozen in time.

The monks, aghast and horrified, were not restricted, and rushed out to call Emergency Services.

Alexa was left writhing on the floor.

The heart still beat and the vision in red entered Alexa's mind, and those of Croxley and Bull Morello.

"Alexa Heléne, your pain and bleeding will now stop. I am she whom you hate so much. I am the Magdalene. Some named me Miriam and others Mary. I am all these and more. I am the companion or wife of beloved, blessed Yeshua, or he whom you name as Jesus. The heart you see beating is that of my devoted and beloved Jacques de Molay, Grand Master of the Templars, who would fight to the death to defend me. I am now beyond that realm, and I owe them so much and will never forget."

Kristy was in tears. "Oh God, what have I done?"

"You saved a life without taking another." The voice was clear and direct. *"For this we are thankful. All of you – your trust and belief have saved his words, written down by me so long ago, for a world now ready to hear them. Return us to our resting place, and we will meet you again at some other time."*

Bella and Kristy were weeping. The two men, not knowing why, had both sunk to one knee with bowed heads before they arose to reassemble the casket and replace the papyrus and de Molay's heart, now still and quiet.

Croxley and his soldiers were still held immobile by an invisible force.

It was not long before the ambulances and armed police arrived. Once they stormed into the shrine room, they saw three people locked in place as if they were statues. Two held firearms and another injured woman was doubled up on the floor. There were four others who looked pleased and joyous

THE MAGDALENE MISSION

to see them. All were ordered to the floor.

It was then Abbot Gregory and Brother Macarius appeared. They had seen a miraculous drama that few would believe.

Chapter 41

The police conducted lengthy interviews with all those involved, including Brother Macarius and Abbot Gregory. They confirmed Isabella's role and that of her team. The Croxley team were charged with kidnapping, grievous bodily harm (GBH), and unlawful possession of firearms – and murder was added, for the death of Bishop Ignatius. The charge against Kristy for causing GBH was quietly ditched. Matthew G. Croxley, Marco 'Bull' Morello, and Alexa Heléne faced long prison sentences.

A task of major importance for Bella was how to handle the delicate matter of the future of the papyrus. She knew the Magdalene papyrus, Jacques de Molay's heart, and the casket belonged to the shrine room, and the last thing she wanted was the separation of de Molay's heart from the papyrus. They belonged together and there was no way she wanted such an event to happen.

Thus, began lengthy discussions with her prestigious library and museum backers and the hierarchy of the Brookwood Church of Saint Edward the Martyr.

Whilst few would believe it, Abbot Gregory had total

THE MAGDALENE MISSION

faith in her. Only he and Brother Macarius knew what she was doing, and they had pledged total secrecy on the matter.

She regularly visited the shrine room, where she communicated with the Magdalene, whose voice and vision would enter her mind.

"Beloved Isabella, we owe you much. Know that there was never a beginning nor will there ever be an end for this universe, of which there are many. These sentiments are in my written words, which you and your friends were so determined to find, and we wanted you to. Your world has changed. There are now so many open minds and, as Yeshua told, some seeds fall on barren soil, others amongst the weeds, and there are some that fall on fertile soil. It was these that blossomed, as indeed you have. We are thankful to you and your companions. Your proposals are accepted."

⚘

They kept their promises to Rabbi Cohen. They told him all they could, and not once did he disbelieve or question the validity of what he was told. He became deeply moved and stated that religions, ultimately, have much to discover and answer for.

They gave him a presentation copy of the papyrus and of Max's translation, telling him his story had inspired them and given them hope.

They were to remain firm friends for the remainder of their lives.

Karl Reinhardt, the curator at the Egyptology Department of the Berlin National Museum, had amicably reached an agreement with the Greek Orthodox Church whereby, every two years, they would borrow the papyrus for a three-month period for all to see and examine on full display.

As the team expected, it was a sensation and had the religious world in a wrenching, divided tailspin not seen since the Dead Sea Scrolls. Articles, books, and the media went into a frenzy of speculation. Not once did Isabella, Max, Kristy, or Jake reveal the true nature of what had really occurred. They would never have been believed and the importance of their discovery would have been ridiculed and devalued. That was never going to happen.

Thirteen Years Later

Kristy and Jake became minor celebrities in the academic fraternity and leading lights in their own field of study and research. They were often pushed to say more, but forever remained tight-lipped about the entire episode. They regarded themselves as blessed and favoured and would never betray the trust of the Magdalene. They never married. They saw no need. They were glued together and no force on earth could ever separate them. Besides, they both had the Magdalene's blessing. As Kristy said, "We saw reality thirteen years back and it has been humbling and moving. I love Jake and he loves me. We have always done so. What else do we need?"

Max and Bella also never married, nor were there any children. The Magdalene episode changed their lives.

THE MAGDALENE MISSION

Max was a new man. All his doubts and misgivings about a spiritual life had evaporated in those last moments he'd witnessed in the shrine room.

He was never the same again.

His relationship with Bella never progressed, although he knew he would do anything she wanted – apart from marriage.

After much soul searching, he applied for a post at Hanazono University in Tokyo. He was accepted – his reputation was well known. It was a private university run by Zen monks of the Rinzai sect in Japan. He knew that was what he wanted, and the Magdalene would approve. Of that he was certain.

Isabella loved Max, but she too had been changed and so had her view of the world. It could never be the same again. She was not surprised at Max's new post and knew it was the right thing for him. She accepted it totally.

The years rolled by, and she retreated from the world and the glare of fame and adulation. Like the others, she never, ever breathed a word of those heady events back then.

All requests for interviews and media were denied and she gave up her lucrative assignments across the board. She began work on a new book, *The Nine Poor Knights of the Temple of Solomon*: *A Quest for the Magdalene.*

Bella became a recluse and shunned all social contact and activities.

But not entirely.

She had a constant companion. The Magdalene spoke to her every day, and she could not wish for anything more. The Magdalene gave her inspiration that she could never gain anywhere on earth.

It was enough for Bella.

She needed nothing more.

And so it was. The team lived out their separate lives.
Not together, but apart.
Forever connected in a strange way… in their love and memories of each other.

Bestselling and multi-award-winning British author, **Ken Fry,** holds a university master's degree in literature.

He has extensive knowledge of the art world. This he acquired while working as a publisher in a major UK publishing house, a wholly owned subsidiary of the HEARST Corp of the USA. In his thirteen years with the company, he worked within the Fine Arts and Antiques division of the organisation and controlled four major international titles.

Fry is known for his captivating storytelling and vivid imagination. His attention to detail and extensive research ensure that readers are fully immersed in the world he has created.

As of this release, Ken Fry has published 21 novels and short stories and 10 audiobooks, and has received several book awards from prestigious award-giving bodies.

He is now retired and devotes his full time to writing. He lives in the UK and shares his home with 'Dickens' his Shetland Sheepdog.

www.booksbykenfry.com
Twitter: @kenfry10

Made in the USA
Middletown, DE
11 June 2023